ending the affair

GRAEME TURNER is Professor of Cultural Studies and Director of the Centre for Critical and Cultural Studies at the University of Queensland. He is one of the key figures in the development of cultural and media studies in Australia and has an outstanding international reputation in the field.

His most recent book is *Understanding Celebrity* (Sage, 2004). Other publications include *The Film Cultures Reader* (Routledge, 2002); (with Stuart Cunningham) *The Media and Communications in Australia* (Allen & Unwin, 2002); (with Frances Bonner and P. David Marshall) *Fame Games: The production of celebrity in Australia* (Cambridge University Press, 2000).

GRAEME TURNER

ending the affair

the decline
of television
current affairs
in Australia

A UNSW Press book

Published by
University of New South Wales Press Ltd
University of New South Wales
Sydney NSW 2052
AUSTRALIA
www.unswpress.com.au

National Library of Australia
Cataloguing-in-Publication entry

   Turner, Graeme.
   Ending the affair: the decline of television current affairs in Australia.

   Includes index.
   ISBN 0 86840 864 6.

   1. Television broadcasting of news – Australia – History.
   2. Television programs – Social aspects – Australia.
   3. Broadcast journalism – Australia – History. I. Title.

   791.45650994

Cover design Di Quick
Text layout Ruth Pidd
Print BPA

Contents

Acknowledgments

The research upon which this book is based was assisted by an Australian Research Council Discovery Grant to investigate the history of Australian television current affairs programming. I would like to acknowledge the research assistance of Sam Searle and Rebecca Farley, who did most of the archival work (and when she got bored, Rebecca did the calculations that told me ten per cent of Australian current affairs hosts have been called Mike). Some of the material which appears in the book has been published in earlier versions in the journals *Media International Australia*, and the *UTS Review*; I would like to thank the editors of these journals for allowing me to draw upon this work and to reproduce some of it in what follows. References to the earlier versions appear in the notes at the end of the chapters concerned. The opening chapter was presented as a plenary address to the 'New(s) Times' conference at the University of Melbourne in 2003, and I would like to thank Simon Cottle for the invitation to present my argument to the conference. I would also like to thank those in attendance who gave me such useful criticism, comments and suggestions, especially Murray Green, Philip Martin, Anne Dunn, David McKnight, and Wendy Bacon.

I would also like to thank Rod Tiffen for encouraging me to have another crack at getting this book published, as well as my editor at UNSW Press, Phillipa McGuinness, for her support (again). Colleagues who have patiently conversed with me on this topic over the years include Frances Bonner, Michael Bromley, Stuart Cunningham, John Hartley, David Marshall and Jason Sternberg. To my wife, Chris, who has had to sit through far too many television news and current affairs programs every night of what must feel like most of her life, my apologies for any damage this may have caused to her perspective on the world. Her support for my work has been a steady and confirming presence over all those years and for that, among many things, I owe her my gratitude.

Preface

*E*nding *the Affair* examines the state of short form[1] television current affairs in Australia today, questioning its future while drawing lessons from the past. The research project from which this book emerged was a history of television current affairs formats in Australia. Funded by the Australian Research Council, its original motivation was to understand the significance of the changes that had occurred in these television formats and their function, particularly since the network upheavals of the late 1980s. *Ending the Affair* draws on that history in order to contextualise the issues being debated in the present. This book also draws on more than ten years of watching, researching, and writing about Australian television current affairs, so that there are parts of this book that have appeared in earlier versions in academic journals. Chapter 2, which deals with the history of ABC TV's *This Day Tonight*, is the only chapter comprised substantially of such material, but two sections of chapter 4 and one section of chapter 6 also use previously published material. Elsewhere, where I have drawn on ideas or arguments that have been published earlier in a different form, I indicate this in the endnotes.

This book is not a comprehensive history of Australian television current affairs, although the arguments it makes certainly have such a history in mind. Rather, what follows is a series of arguments, provoked largely by the current situation and its attendant debates, and focused on the programs and points in time most relevant to the argument being made. Consequently, I will not discuss in detail every program or shift in format, and I deal only in passing with the contribution made by the SBS, for instance. For the most part, I have chosen to concentrate on the commercial free-to-air networks and the ABC as the most significant forces in the Australian television market today. My historical focus is upon the years since the late 1980s when the development of the national commercial networks changed the conditions under which television current affairs was produced and consumed. The historical spread, nonetheless, is as broad as possible: the book discusses the pioneering *This Day Tonight*, which commenced in 1967, as well as current programs such as *A Current Affair* and alternative platforms such as those provided by pay TV and the Internet. The analysis is contextualised, too, against the industrial and regulatory conditions within which Australian television current affairs has been produced.

The book proceeds from an ethical orientation that questions the social and political value of what we now think of as television current affairs journalism in Australia. Current affairs programs remain a staple component of the evening schedule for most channels in Australia and, together with news, they are routinely considered as among the most important sectors of the industry when regulatory authorities inquire into the provision of broadcasting services to the Australian community. From time to time, it will be necessary for me to talk about television news as well, as sometimes it is difficult to disentangle the two. Jointly, news and current affairs carry the responsibility of providing the information component of free-to-air broadcasting; as a result, no matter how the formats mutate, they remain among the central elements of the nation's broadcast television system. This is because, most of us would agree, television news and current affairs programs serve functions that are fundamentally important to a civilised democracy. Therefore, if the contemporary versions of television current affairs are not serving such functions – and if there is nothing else which *is* – then *Ending the Affair* argues that this is significant cause for concern.

Those who work in the television industry are often, perhaps understandably, annoyed at criticism, from commentators, academics or the public, which in their view reveals an ignorance of the conditions under which their work has to be performed. In what follows, I certainly seek, respect, and take account of industry points of view. However, I also believe that this particular form of programming is too important to leave entirely to the industry – or, indeed, entirely to the mechanisms of the market. Given that free-to-air proprietors operate a highly lucrative but scarce natural resource while being protected from the introduction of new competitors, and given that the ABC is funded by our taxes – albeit, perhaps, by not enough – there is a contract of civic responsibility and obligation in place that needs to be invoked more than it has been recently.

Here, then, is a series of arguments about Australian television current affairs programming, aimed at encouraging greater public scrutiny of its current performance as well as a greater awareness of the histories which have brought us to the position we now occupy.

Graeme Turner
Brisbane

NOTE

1   'Short form' refers to (typically) 30-minute programs composed of a number of items; 'long form' programs usually deal with one story in a single 45- to 50-minute edition.

CHAPTER ONE

Television current affairs: does it have a future?

Format fatigue: the decline of television current affairs

Once it was one of the flagship television formats, filling in the background to the news and serving as a key location for network identity, for the discharge of television's public information responsibilities, and for shaping public debate. Current affairs has been among the highest rating formats on broadcast television and individual editions still turn up in the top ten programs for the week. Today, however, few would deny that it is well past its golden years. At the ABC, current affairs has never returned to the dizzy heights reached during the late 1960s and early 1970s when the pioneering *This Day Tonight* (TDT) regularly won its timeslot and turned presenters such as Bill Peach and Peter Luck into stars. Commercial television current affairs programming had its own halcyon days during the late 1980s and early 1990s, then attracting the kind of public attention now reserved for scrutinising reality-TV shows. Their major stars – George Negus, Jana Wendt, Michael Willesee and Ray Martin – were featured on the covers of mass market magazines from *TV Week* to the *Australian Women's Weekly* and the release of the line-up and format for each new show was a major media story.

At the end of the 1980s the Australian television industry was experiencing the consequences of the most dramatic ownership upheaval in its history. With networks changing hands for inflated prices and the advertising dollar shrinking, everyone was in trouble and current affairs programs were one of the places where management sought salvation. In Australia, the 6.00–7.30 pm timeslot has long been regarded as the platform upon which to build the audience for the rest of the night. Try as they might, none of the networks' strategies for building this timeslot into the 1990s worked for long; millions were spent in what turned out to be a period of great activity and innovation. At the quality end of the market, Ten's *Page One* and its successor *Public Eye* attracted attention in 1988 and 1989 for poaching a large number of the ABC's *Four Corners* reporting personnel: Chris Masters, Kerry O'Brien, and Maxine McKew among them. When the *Four Corners* model didn't work, Ten changed gears and injected even more hype into its week-nightly *Hinch* and Gordon Elliott's one-hour weekly *Hard Copy* in 1991 – the latter was probably the first unashamedly tabloid current affairs program on Australian television. At Seven, ex-*This Day Tonight* original and the founding producer of *Sixty Minutes*, Gerald Stone, returned to Australia from the US to produce *Real Life* in 1992, announcing his intention of beating *A Current Affair* at its own game. These major interventions by the Seven and Ten networks were aimed at emulating the ratings success of what were then, the mar-ket leaders – the Nine Network's long-running programs *Sixty Minutes* and *A Current Affair*.

This level of investment and invention simply couldn't be sustained. By the mid-1990s, the current affairs ratings bubble had well and truly burst. The commercial networks' last serious attempt to develop a new prime time quality 'public affairs' program, Seven's *Witness*, went to air in 1996 and struggled through various dramas and timeslots before foundering in a welter of good intentions, poor ratings and accusations of bad faith in 1998. In fact, and notwithstanding the best attempts of the network programmers, the audiences for short form[1] television current affairs have been declining for more than a decade. While we can see far more news than ever before, there are fewer examples of the current affairs format available on television today than there were fifteen years ago. Analysis of the format's decline has become a staple item of media commentary in recent years (see, for example, the number of articles from *The Australian's*

Media supplement which turn up in the list of references for this book).

The audiences for television current affairs are not only declining, they are also ageing; the demographics for these programs 'skew old', with an audience dominated by the over-50s. In fact, research suggests that young people are actively repelled by, not just uninterested in, current examples of the format (Evans and Sternberg, 2000; Sternberg, 2002; Sternberg, 2004). A striking feature of the late 1990s was the number of comedy and satiric programs which pitched to a youth audience by parodying mainstream news and current affairs formats and programs: *Fast Forward, Full Frontal, Good News Week, The Late Report,* and, more recently, *CNNNN* and *The Chaser* (Plane, 1999). There are intimations of revenge in this. Not only are young people alienated from prime-time current affairs because they find it visually boring, narrowly conservative in the range of points of view it canvasses, and dependent upon anchor persons with little appeal to their age-group, but they also resent the fact that such programs routinely treat youth culture as an object of derision, moral panic, or prurience. Increasingly, this younger demographic is finding its news and current affairs content in other formats – comedy/chat shows such as *The Panel,* or *The Glasshouse,* for example.

Contemporary Australian prime-time current affairs formats look increasingly tired and aimless, working over the same territory as each other with ever-diminishing returns. This is no secret, but is routinely picked up for comment in other media:

> Across the nation the 6.30 pm commercial current affairs programs [are] giving their viewers their daily dose of what has become staple fare: consumer and lifestyle stories sprinkled with a little traditional current affairs and spiced up with trashy fillers that wouldn't be out of place in a racy supermarket mag such as *The National Enquirer.*
>
> Some of the items, usually four in each half hour, are seen on a regular basis: back pain, shonky tradesmen, diets, plastic surgery, home renovations, budgeting and the ubiquitous neighborhood dispute are regular themes. (Meade, 2002)

As such reports usually point out, looking 'behind the news' is a thing of the past, and the ritual grilling of politicians has been left to an increasingly worn-looking Kerry O'Brien on *The 7.30 Report.* According to Amanda

Meade's 2002 story on the banality of current affairs programs I have quoted from above, it had been a whole year since Seven's *Today Tonight* had interviewed the prime minister, John Howard. In his place ran the endless, promo-driven stories on celebrities, lifestyle, and consumer complaints.

The similarity of the programming strategies adopted by Seven and Nine is all the more surprising because they have done nothing to arrest the decline in audience numbers or the rising cynicism with which the programs are regarded by the public. Nonetheless, as the audiences turn off, the competition for those remaining intensifies. What this competition produces in terms of newsgathering practices lies on the bottom of the ethical gene pool: largely, those arrogant and dishonest practices targeted so mercilessly in the ABC's mid-90s satiric series, *Frontline*. As *Frontline's* success must indicate, audiences are aware of these practices and increasingly register their distrust of the programs and their reporters through the complaints procedures of FACTS (Federation of Australian Commercial Television Stations)[2] – despite the fact that these procedures are themselves effectively designed to protect the interests of the networks.[3] It is not surprising, therefore, that the complaints don't have much effect. Consequently, contemporary current affairs programs continue to employ a range of tactics that are as questionable as they are ubiquitous:

> Generally, the tools of the trade are taken for granted: hidden cameras to entrap people, money to entice others, staged 'walk-ins' to humiliate the people cast as the bad guys, traps set to catch allegedly shonky businessmen and people not always told the truth about the reason for the interview. (Meade, 1999: 2–3)

As a result of such tactics feeding the audience's cynicism about the format, there is now serious doubt within the television production industry about television current affairs' long-term prospects. Therefore it is appropriate to examine the current situation with these programs before asking if television current affairs formats have a future and, if they do, what might that future look like.

'The big turn-off': the disappearing audience

A place to start is with the audience. Studies of the decline in news and current affairs audiences have been conducted in a number of countries. The Australian study that showed the most dramatic results was produced by Jon Casimir (1998) and it focused on the total audience numbers (not the ratings) for prime-time news and current affairs programming in Sydney between 1991 and 1998. Casimir provided evidence of a substantial decline in news and current affairs audiences across the whole market. The current affairs figures were alarming. Over the period surveyed, *Four Corners* had dropped 44.7 per cent of its audience; *A Current Affair* had dropped 29.2 per cent; *The 7.30 Report* had dropped 27.3 per cent. The figures for news were bad for the commercial leaders, but nonetheless suggestive because they supported a view that some market diversity might be in order: the Nine Network's evening news dropped 23.1 per cent, but ABC news gained 11.1 per cent and the Ten Network's early news increased its numbers by 19.6 per cent. What had seemed at the time a slightly desperate move – Ten's abandoning the 6.00 pm timeslot to the competition in order to opt for an untried timeslot of 5.00 pm and a one-hour bulletin – had proved highly successful and Casimir's figures demonstrated that. Although Casimir's report has not been updated, many of the trends he highlighted have sharpened since. Despite the race downmarket by the two commercial programs that was intended to address precisely this situation, the market leader, *A Current Affair*, went on to lose more than 25 per cent of its national audience between 1999 and 2002, going from two million to 1.49 million (Meade, 2002: 4). Currently, according to the most recent ratings figures as I write, it is tracking at around 1.2 million per week (although with significant variations from week to week – itself an indication that brand loyalty is slipping).

This is not unique to Australia. In the US, too, audiences are abandoning broadcast network news and current affairs programming as the majority now draw their news and information from cable news services, or from entertainment programming – late-night talk shows such as those hosted by David Letterman and Jay Leno – or they simply take no news at all. West and Orman suggest that roughly 10 per cent of Americans get their news from late-night entertainment programs like those fronted by Letterman or Leno; significantly, they point out, for those under thirty years of age, this proportion climbs to 'nearly half' (2003: 100).

In the UK, a recent study funded by the Independent Television Commission (the ITC) found that only 16 per cent of those surveyed included any current affairs among their regular viewing, and the researchers expressed alarm at the 'sharp decline' in audiences for this form of programming; current affairs, they concluded, 'seems to have lost its place as a regular appointment to view television' (Hargreaves and Thomas, 2002: 6). They quoted Richard Sambrook, Director of News at the BBC, who noted that 'regular, in-depth current affairs series in prime time have all but disappeared in British television' (6). The study revealed patterns in current affairs content similar to those also apparent in Australia: consumer affairs, scandal, and celebrity stories had increased in importance, while politics and social issues had taken a back seat.[4] Interestingly, the UK researchers blamed more than the media for this, and one of their recommendations was addressed to party politicians, urging them to 'urgently reconsider those respects in which their media behaviour discourages public interest in politics' (8).

The UK study examined news as well as current affairs and their findings are more equivocal about the former than they are about the latter format. On the one hand, shifts in the news agenda had reduced the coverage of politics largely in favour of the coverage of crime (something which is replicated in Australia); and the staple news diet was increasingly influenced by stories on personalities or celebrities (again, repeated in Australia). On the other hand, as a result of the spread of subscription services, the amount of news available to the public had actually increased significantly (an eightfold increase in hours per week between 1986 and 1997). In addition, and notwithstanding the shifts in content and approach, the authors argued that British television 'still supplies a broadly serious news agenda' (18). News audiences were nonetheless in decline. The report quoted from Sambrook's address to the Royal Television Society in 2001, where he referred to a growing disaffection with the news among young people, while also pointing to the alarming fact that this disaffected group seemed to be getting older: where once it was the under-25s who did not watch the news, now it was the under-35s.

'If we don't do something', he said, 'in 10 years time it will be the under-55s and then the under-65s who don't watch the news' (Hargreaves and Thomas, 2002: 11).

For current affairs, though, the UK evidence is unequivocally worrying. In terms of audience interest in the format, the figures are compelling: '[B]etween 1994-2001, the current affairs audience fell by 31.7 per cent: down from 64.3 hours per year in 1994 to 43.9 in 2001, and dropped to 15 hours for the first six months of 2002' (25).[5] From the industry's point of view, Hargreaves and Thomas reported, current affairs is 'a genre in crisis, with no regular series left in peak-time, resulting in a growing shortage of trained current affairs producers for the strands that do exist' (20). While the researchers shared the concern about the reduced capacity this represents, they also expressed scepticism about how genuinely the industry had attempted to satisfy the public's core interests in the format. They commented that the broadcasters' withdrawal from current affairs 'seems to be at odds with some opinion research which suggests the public values highly documentary current affairs and factual programming, if not quite as highly as news itself' (20). The implication is that there is a market for this format, but that broadcasters have failed to supply it.

There are many contextual issues here. The disappearance of the youth audience, for instance, is widely noted in all markets, but particularly in the UK, the US and Australia. David Mindich, the author of *Tuned Out: Why young people don't follow the news* (2004), has pointed out that only a tiny fraction of the four hours per day television consumed by young people in the US is news. Entertainment programs and the Internet – while the latter is not as substantial an influence as sometimes suggested – are leaching away youth audiences from traditional news media (if not from traditional news content).

The ITC report also accepted that the lack of interest in political content in news and current affairs may not necessarily be the result of the dumbing down of news and information services, but may in fact reflect wider social trends:

In the 2001 General Election in Britain, turnout was 59.4%, the lowest since 1918 and the worst since women got the vote; turnout peaked in 1954 at 84%. Among 18–25 year-olds, turnout was even lower (39%) and British Social Attitudes data suggests that by 1999, only one in 10 among this age group considered itself 'quite' or 'very interested' in politics, compared with one in five in 1986. (Hargreaves and Thomas, 2002: 9)

While we don't have a comparable set of statistics in Australia, given compulsory voting, it is likely that these general trends would be reflected here too, supporting the view that there is a declining interest in politics in our society. Against that kind of possibility, though, other sources are quoted in the ITC study which argue that the ratings figures for election broadcasts suggest that the population is suffering from a lack of information *about* politics, rather than lack of interest or apathy (Hargreaves and Thomas, 2002: 9). The BBC was sufficiently worried about these issues to commission a study by Sean Kevill which focused directly on people's disillusionment with politics. Among other things, he argued that people were not uninterested or disengaged with the political *per se* but, rather, were disillusioned specifically with mainstream politics and the way it is played out in the media (see Kevill, 2002).

The commercial conditions in which the various media systems operate vary significantly from market to market, and from country to country. In Australia, there are specific conditions which have contributed to the situation being described. In particular, the panic-stricken competition which occurred at the end of the 1980s had its foundation in a series of government policy initiatives as well as in some bizarre commercial decisions. The aggregation of the markets for regional television stations, the high prices paid when each of the networks changed hands in the ownership upheaval of the late 1980s, the formal creation of the three big national television networks, and the rapid escalation of costs in the radio industry as a result of the implementation of the first stages of the National Radio Plan, all contributed to a dramatic heightening of competition for the national advertising dollar – a competition which was played out in the contest for ratings. For a variety of reasons, this intensified competition reconfirmed and emphasised the importance of the national current affairs program as the network flagship. Not only that, but since it was then believed that news and current affairs could be a ratings winner, and that there was no need to assess their performance any differently to other formats – that is, to protect their public information role – the unchallenged indicator of the programs' success as network flagships was their audience ratings.

The establishment of the national networks had the long-term tendency of replacing the local audience with the national audience. This in turn had the effect of disconnecting commercial television from some of the obligations for community service and accountability which had hitherto operated, no matter how imperfectly or contestably. From the industry's point of view, there was much to gain from networking. It provided economies of scale in production and delivery and it facilitated the maintenance of consistency of quality and approach in programming. Furthermore, the decline in profits which had accompanied the industry's restructuring injected these benefits with great urgency. However, the economic logic did not easily translate into marketing and programming logic. Where individual channels might have built their reputation upon a local identity – the Perth stations, for instance, were all in this category – the network now required a corporate identity which was national. The pressure on the flagship news and current affairs programs to find new ways to create this identity, maintain it, and thus deliver audiences into prime time entertainment, was increased. One suspects, however, that national programs – particularly once the industry agrees that federal politics does not attract an audience – are a little more difficult to design. Stories which address and interest audiences in all regions are hard to find. Ultimately, the idealistic hope of finding a 'multi-local' audience had to give way to the real necessity of constructing a new, national audience. The consequent ferocity of the competition in television that marked the 1990s provided the conditions within which flagship formats would compete head-to-head, with no holds barred. The puzzling point, perhaps, is why the news and current affairs formats focused on competing against each other in such a headlong sprint downmarket. Why didn't this competition produce some upmarket ventures as well?

One answer is to point to programs such as *Page One* (Ten) and *Witness* (Seven), which certainly did attempt to provide quality 'public affairs', and failed to hold their audience. There are not many other examples of this, however. Overwhelmingly, the networks' default position was to move towards the populist agenda of the so-called tabloid format; so, in an extreme illustration of this, when *Page One* failed, the Ten Network turned to *Hard Copy*. The networks argue that this is where their ratings were driving them, but it is hard to read the history of these ratings as unequivocally supporting such a claim. One possibility may be that the success of talkback radio – which had already taken up residence at the bottom end of the market – supported the view that a large mass audience could be reached via that route. Certainly, the demotic flavour that talkback developed over the 1980s and 1990s could be tasted in the approaches taken in commercial television current affairs at that time. More directly, talkback's success was obviously the rationale for the direct appropriation of two of the key talkback radio figures – Derryn Hinch and Alan Jones – as hosts of their own nightly current affairs programs on networks Seven and Ten, and the remaining big name, John Laws, as the host of his own chat show on Foxtel.[6]

The 'post-journalism' environment

A further consideration could be encapsulated under the general heading of 'post-journalism' – a phrase coined, I believe, by Altheide and Snow in 1991, although there are a number of other locations where it appears, seemingly for the first time, during the 1990s (for example, in my own article (Turner, 1996c) which forms the basis for much of chapter 4). As I will outline in more detail in chapter 4, the phrase 'post-journalism' refers to the factors underlying shifts in the industrial production of news which have the effect of nudging the journalist aside in order to exploit other, less independent, sources of information. The growth of public relations, the reduction in the news media's resourcing of news gathering – both in terms of personnel and funds – and the increased competition between news media has reinforced the importance of controlling access to, as well as the supply and presentation of, news stories. Buying the exclusive rights to stories has become an established practice; to accomplish this, the news media must deal with agents, managers and publicists before they gain access to their news sources. Over the last two decades, publicity, promotion and public relations have become just as integral to the practices of commercial news production as to the marketing and positioning of the commercial media organisation itself.

In my view it is now undeniable that news and current affairs content is as much the product of public relations and publicity as of journalism. In the research which was published in *Fame Games* (Turner et al., 2000), my co-authors and I outlined the growth of the public relations and publicity industries since the 1980s, and argued that they are now responsible for a significant proportion of media content right across the various sectors. In the mass market magazine sector, where one might of course expect the influence of the publicity industry to feed a heightened interest in celebrity, it is the single most dominant category of story.[7] Within current affairs programming on television, celebrity stories accounted for between 30 and 50 per cent of the story topics on some of the programs surveyed: these included the market leaders *A Current Affair* and *Sixty Minutes*. However, the influence of public relations is not confined to celebrity or entertainment stories. Tracking the fate of government public relations media releases – determining their success rate in being published, uncorroborated or without any significant change – has revealed alarming results; one study found that, in television, 60 per cent of these media releases were taken up and used without any corroboration at all (Turner et al., 2000: 42). Given that kind of result, it is not hard to credit assessments which suggest that between 70 per cent and 80 per cent of the content of our newspapers originates in media releases from public relations firms or personnel (Turner et al., 2000: 40–43).

The effect of government public relations units upon the content and treatment of news is not simply the result of the strategic intervention of spin doctors. Rather, the *Fame Games* research suggested, it is a routine operation of government that is just as routinely accepted by a news media hungry for stories and too busy to question everything that lands on their desks. Perhaps less obviously, it is also worth pointing out that the business press is probably the worst example of a sector of news which is almost entirely in the capture of its sources. Surveys of the output of the business sections of the print media have found an extraordinary proportion of business news has been lifted, unchanged, from the press releases of the companies concerned. Clara Zawawi's 1994 research, which we discuss in *Fame Games*, found that between 84 per cent (*Sydney Morning Herald*) and 93 per cent (*Australian*) of the business news published in our quality papers was composed of little more than public relations releases. Small wonder that the fall of HIH or One.Tel came as such surprises to the Australian consumer. While Zawawi is at pains to point out that her interest is in locating the effects of changes in journalism's work practices, resource allocation and management direction rather than anything more sinister, and although her research involves the print media only, she does make the concluding comment that perhaps we should remove the journalist 'from the centre of the news process in the print media and give more emphasis to the role of the public relations practitioner' (1994: 70–71).

Zawawi's comments remain worthy of serious attention because the shifts in journalistic practice and in the conditions within which journalists have to work should not be left out of the equation here. The intensity of the commercial competition described earlier has increased the pressure on individual journalists to come up with the goods on a regular basis. This, at a time when the downsizing and casualising of newsrooms has reduced journalists' capacity for investigative work and enforced the prioritisation of 'same day' stories. As each medium attempts to exploit its industrial edge in order to beat the competition, we find that the electronic media increasingly look to exploit immediacy as one of their preferred means of competing with the print media. This has significantly increased the speed of the daily news cycle for these media, and thus reduced the time available for checking facts or for corroboration. The print media are caught between two strategies as they attempt to respond: to go for more detail and more depth (the broadsheet option), on the one hand; or to opt for colour, shock-horror teasers, sensationalist headlines and pictures, and multiple editions (the tabloid option), on the other hand. Some outlets do both – offering competing versions of journalism within the one publication in order to protect their circulations against an increasing number of competing media.

In the midst of all this, it has to be acknowledged that those dedicated (or privileged) few who do manage to perform investigative journalism in the traditional manner do not find it a comfortable occupation. Anyone who has heard *Four Corners* journalist Chris Masters speak in the last few years will have heard him say that the ten years of litigation he endured after the broadcast of his *Four Corners* story on corruption in the Queensland police, 'The Moonlight State', was simply not worth it. This is a clear example of a story which had enormous social and political repercussions, and has changed the nature of Queensland politics. Yet, the person who was responsible for it has been so ruthlessly hounded through the courts that he now says publicly that if he had known what lay ahead he would not have done it. The use of stop-writs, libel and defamation actions has been increasing, particularly as a means by which large organisations or corporations can prevent publication. Australian journalists have long argued that the nature of the libel and defamation laws in Australia, and the fact that they vary significantly across state jurisdictions, has actively assisted those who are the legitimate object of public investigation. At present, multilateral negotiations are underway to produce a set of national defamation laws, which might exclude corporations as eligible complainants and which could establish truth as a complete defence – neither of which is the case at present. Such changes would improve the conditions under which the investigative end of journalism might operate. The fact that the federal government and the Media, Arts and Entertainment Alliance are negotiating on this process at the moment does indicate how seriously it has been taken (and progress reports on these negotiations indicate how difficult it will be to satisfy the competing interests involved).[8] This also reminds us that the commercial pressures facing media organisations are not solely those involved in beating their competitors to the story; it also involves absorbing the legal costs of a story once it has been published. Understanding this helps to explain why the kinds of stories for which Masters became famous – most of which date back into the 1980s and early 1990s now[9] – are now simply not commissioned by the commercial networks,[10] and only rarely by the ABC or SBS.

'News entertainment' and politics

The really depressing thing is that these intensely competitive media systems are fighting over something the public seems less and less bothered about: that is, news. The category of news itself, and in particular the 'behind the news' model of current affairs, looks increasingly old-fashioned. Journalism finds itself backed into something of a corner. Under the pressure of marketplace competition, journalism has increasingly opted to define itself, in effect if not always explicitly, as a form of entertainment rather than information. It has taken some time to do this, and the early attempts met with significant consumer resistance as well as with the difficulties in calibrating innovations in the format. When comedian and talk-show host Graham Kennedy hosted a hybrid late news and comedy program in the 1980s, called *Graham Kennedy's News Show*, the mix of information and entertainment formats proved a little uncontrollable. Reading the news for laughs simply offended people. The format was eventually revised and renamed *Graham Kennedy Coast to Coast*, Kennedy stopped reading the news himself and a live audience was brought into the studio to make it clear that we were meant to laugh at the jokes (I deal with this in greater length in chapter 4, below). In the UK, the salacious tabloid red-top newspaper, *Sunday Sport*, legitimated its practice of printing totally fictional stories in a news format by calling itself a 'news entertainment' on its masthead, rather than a newspaper.

In American television, what is usually nominated as the most significant moment in the shift away from news to entertainment occurred during the 1970s when the success of *60 Minutes* proved, for the first time in that market, that current affairs could achieve top ratings. The practice employed by the US networks at that time, of quarantining news and current affairs programming from the ratings as a means of protecting the provision of public information, appeared no longer to be necessary. Since then, it seems in hindsight, news and current affairs programming has increasingly been forced to conceive of the competition for audiences as a competition over the provision of entertainment rather than merely of accurate and useful information. This has produced the shifts in the format's content we have seen over the last two decades: the introduction of sport, personality and celebrity gossip, for instance, as well as consumer affairs stories.

It has produced shifts in method, too. Ethically questionable tactics such as the use of hidden cameras have displaced more conventional investigative journalism as a means of exploiting television's capacity for dramatic visual exposure and revelation. There have been knock-on effects. By compromising the legitimacy of some of its methods, the authority of the program and ultimately of the format became increasingly dependent upon the credibility of the constructed persona of the presenter/host. Along the way, journalist Amanda Meade has pointed out, 'the notion that the programs should follow the daily news, providing current affairs reports and interviewing key players, has all but evaporated' (2002: 4).

An acknowledged casualty of such an approach is the treatment of politics. In Australia, politics has largely been evacuated from commercial television current affairs, although it survives in diminished form (largely) as a ritualised Q&A exchange on the ABC. There are very few long-term investigations mounted and very little use of investigative research as a means of framing a political or social issue. As noted earlier, it is commonplace to point out that most commercial current affairs programs employ a narrow range of populist story topics (back pain, cellulite, cosmetic surgery, difficult neighbours) and are loath to deal with politicians at all. The allocation of resources is also implicated here – most starkly in the 7.30 *Report's* routine attempt to cover national politics via a live conversation between the host and the relevant correspondent rather than through filmed stories or direct reporting from a range of sources. When the program does interrogate a political representative, mostly it is without the support of any specialised investigative research and so the resulting product is an entirely ritualised performance of the participants' respective roles. Where once the coverage of politics might have been regarded as a fundamental media responsibility, for a range of reasons wider than I will go into at this point, that is no longer the case. This is a deliberate and strategic choice for the commercial networks. The argument routinely offered by the likes of news and current affairs veteran Peter Meakin (formerly of Nine Network, now at Seven) is that the public is simply not interested in politics and that any show which put long interviews with politicians to air would be cutting its own throat, in terms of ratings (Meade, 1999: 3). Any suggestion to the contrary is, we are told, simply wrong.

This explanation has been around for a long time (it appears in the ITC report as well, in the conversations with current affairs producers [see Hargreaves and Thomas, 2002: 99]). It is not simply self-serving. Clearly, something like it must have informed those earlier regimes of programming which quarantined news and current affairs from the commercial effects of poor ratings in order to ensure that they continued to deliver information to the public. Furthermore, it would seem to be supported by Australian media commentators and pundits such as Hugh Mackay who, for instance, regrets what he suggests is the public's apparent apathy about, or disengagement from, politics over the last decade or so (see Mackay, 1999). As we have seen already, this is a familiar argument, both sides of which are canvassed in the ITC study referred to earlier in this chapter. Nevertheless, I am not convinced that what Mackay describes constitutes a cause of the character of the contemporary media's representation of politics. Rather, I think it may be an effect. Specifically, I am sceptical about the claim's validity as a general principle to account for the contemporary interests of the media audience, particularly when I look at other media formats where politics has proved to be a fundamental component over a very long time – such as metropolitan talkback radio, where it is the staple diet. I argue in chapter 2 that there are reasons to regard this, today, as a convenient justification for avoiding content areas likely to offend powerful interests or institutions upon whom the program or the network may some time in the future depend – such as those involved in funding (the ABC) or in protection from commercially damaging regulatory changes (the commercials).

To foreshadow part of the argument made in chapter 2, which deals with the classic Australian television current affairs program, *This Day Tonight*, I suggest that *TDT* was closed down for a number of reasons, and prominent among them was its history of attracting political pressure to the ABC's management. The history of *TDT* was one of regular controversy; the management of the ABC at that time was strongly inclined to co-operate with government and in many instances responded to government pressure by disciplining program staff – in some cases pressuring them to leave. At the end of its eleven-year run, *TDT* was still enjoying ratings that today's *7.30 Report* would kill for, but all its highest profile staff – both in front of and behind the camera – had left the program. Those who remained were burnt out, the anecdotal evidence from former staff would suggest, to a great extent by the demands of continually defending their decisions and their colleagues. ABC management regarded the program as a hot potato, too difficult an operation to maintain, and sought reasons to close it down.

TDT's distinction was that it popularised politics as a new form of content for Australian television. Its success provoked the Seven Network to poach *TDT*'s Michael Willesee (significantly, himself the object of pressure from ABC management for his interviewing style), to launch the first generation of *A Current Affair*. The reputation of *ACA* at Seven was built around the Willesee interview – long, searching, skilled interviews with politicians and public figures (and, eventually, celebrities). Comparisons with the contemporary version of the program only serve to reinforce the possibility that today's audiences are not actually bored with politics at all. Rather, perhaps, they have been bored and alienated by the diminution of the journalistic strategies employed in the media's contemporary performance and representation of politics.

Rarely is a television current affairs interview used as an occasion to spring a surprise – to introduce new information the journalist has uncovered independently and about which the interviewee has not been warned. Where this does happen, it is usually as part of a process used to ensnare the small-time operator – the tradesman or shonky salesman. (The last time I saw it happen in a political interview was when *Lateline's* Tony Jones asked Health Minister Tony Abbott about his meeting with Cardinal George Pell – and it certainly livened up that exchange!) Regrettably, today, the political interview has become institutionally integrated into the public ritual of party politics; one might suggest that the continuing relationship between the program and the politician has become more important – to both parties – than the production of journalism or the generation of news on that day. It goes without saying that producers of television current affairs programs have actively collaborated in this process. And it is not hard to understand why. Once a program's capacity to generate political pressure becomes a significant practical problem for the network it is not surprising that management would prefer to draw the format's teeth.

The treatment of politics then becomes wrapped in the recent industrial history of the medium and of the format. While the story of what has happened to the format at the ABC is slightly different – although by no means unaffected by the kinds of influences I am describing here – what I have been presenting so far is largely a tale of the effect of the commercialisation of the news service. The scale of the commercialisation of the format, with the regularisation of such practices as cheque-book journalism; the effect of deregulation on television's responsibility for informing the public by no longer requiring the media to properly resource the reporting of social and political issues; and the responses of those in charge of television news and current affairs to these changes and pressures, are interrelated contingencies that have produced the current situation: where current affairs must now be considered an endangered format.

Bigger pictures: the industrial context and its ramifications

Of course, and as I have acknowledged earlier on, none of this is peculiar to the Australian context. What I am dealing with here is just a small chapter in a larger story of what has happened to television as a medium over the last decade or two as a result of competing and/or converging media systems, globalising western media industries, and the widespread prevalence of neoliberal policy frameworks for intranational media and cultural regulatory (or, more accurately, de-regulatory) regimes. In general terms, there is an uneven trend for television systems worldwide to migrate from public to private ownership, as governments increasingly opt to move from a regulatory to a deregulatory environment – often invoking the incapacity of national policy to maintain control over a convergent and globalising media system. (There are plenty of exceptions to this, however, and New Zealand offers the one example of which I am aware where a media regulatory system has embraced the challenge of 're–regulating'.[11]) What this has meant at the level of the television format is that it has assisted television to shift its focus from addressing national communities and towards addressing 'taste communities'. As the availability of channels and modes of delivery proliferate, and as television formats migrate from an information to an entertainment function, the industry's conception of the audience has had to shift from the mass market to the niche market. To date, this shift is still a minority one in Australia – we are still attempting to construct the national audience. The evidence from other places – particularly where there is significant penetration of pay TV – suggests this is only a matter of time.

As a result, the days of the national networked free-to-air audience are numbered. Increasingly, we can expect to see the national audience currently addressed by our news and current affairs programs give way either to more localised or more globalised constructions of the audience. A consequence of this, already in train in other spheres of culture, will be the repositioning of the addressee of television as a consumer of programming or commodities, rather than as a citizen of the nation state. To maintain a national conversation about politics through television, then, is going to require some commitment and imagination as the focus of commercial development moves from national to global markets.

That's not the whole story, however. While these industrial trends might suggest the future for national-based current affairs is very limited, the trends in programming formats would suggest otherwise. On the evidence of the growth of reality TV, lifestyle programming, and the redefinition of documentary that has come (ironically) from programming such as *Big Brother*, suggest the balance of power – in terms of dominant formats and audience interest – is currently moving from 'representation' to 'reality'. That is, the potential of television is increasingly located in its perceived capacity to bring us 'the real' unmediated, not its representation. As a result, and while virtually all the reality-television programs which aim to do this are organised in traditionally narrativised forms (the soap opera, for example, is the dominant mode in most), we may be witnessing a revival of the genre of the documentary at the expense of the dramatic narrative. Such a revival can only be assisted by the concurrent fashion of television's preferred subject matter – the focus on 'the ordinary', rather than the extraordinary (see Bonner, 2003).

These are major industrial and commercial shifts, that are widespread internationally and difficult for any individual producer to resist. They do not only affect news and current affairs. In what ways, then, are there specific ramifications for news and current affairs? First, the ramifications do not emerge from the mutations of genre or format that have taken current affairs slowly towards becoming a genre of entertainment which simply makes use of news-related material. Rather, the ramifications are related to the special function that news and current affairs have assumed—and from the kinds of legitimacy these formats can claim to retain that are the historical residue of their earlier public role—as information services crucial to the operation of democracy. The changes in format I have been describing, as well as their targeting of a populist audience and their everyday concerns, do impact on this earlier conception of the format's public utility.

Not surprisingly, most of those in charge of current affairs programming – certainly this is true of those in commercial networks in Australia – are extremely defensive about these changes. Some deny that they have occurred at all, or if they have occurred that this is simply a matter of keeping up with the times· 'they [current affairs programs] haven't taken a different turn, they have just evolved', says Today Tonight's executive producer, Craig McPherson. 'If you're talking traditional current affairs from a decade ago, you would say times have changed, and you've got to keep up with the times' (Meade, 2002: 4.). Others argue that they have no choice if they don't want to 'bore the pants off people', to quote Peter Meakin (Meade, 1999: 3). Meakin defended A Current Affair's treatment of the notorious Paxtons stories[12] by saying that '[I]t was a very valid story; I wish we could do it again' – essentially a journalist's defence. However, he also expressed irritation that the aspiration to be entertaining had apparently become so disreputable ('[why is] entertainment such a dirty word?' [Meade, 1999: 2]) – essentially a commercial defence. If it were not for the dubious claims to journalistic 'validity', in my view, the imperative of being entertaining would not be a problem. But this is a routine move: the public wants to be entertained, the producers say, and so they will entertain them. If this means targeting small-time conmen, frauds and fakes – with the occasional innocent party being caught in the net – so be it. No-one wants to see politicians any more, no-one wants to be bored, and these stories still enable the producers to claim they are continuing to fulfill their socio-political role as the public's advocate.

This is a highly contentious set of rationales for a most important genre of programming, where the rationales, it seems to me, do matter. What concerns me is that a genre of entertainment has evolved which still wants to invoke its journalistic origins as a means of legitimation. At the same time, the advocates for the genre also point out the naïvety of using purely journalistic judgments to influence their commercial strategy or indeed in making the daily decisions which implement their format. Or, to put it another way, the producers of commercial current affairs programs defend their traditional social function through the invocation of their rhetorical commitment to journalism. On the other hand, they also argue that it is commercially naïve to complain about the *highly selective* nature of their practical commitments to journalism. As the welter of media critiques of this compromised defense would suggest, this doesn't convince anybody any more. One of the reasons for this is that we know – in this format above all – that these commercial decisions have human consequences. Television comic John Safran outraged ACA's Ray Martin by putting this directly to Martin's face – performing a classic ACA surprise walk-in on Martin at home. He was there with a camera to meet Martin and his wife as they returned with the shopping one morning, accompanied by 'dole bludger' Shane Paxton who insisted that Martin account for the damage he and his program had done, so gratuitously, to Paxton's family. Not so pleased with being at the other end of his own program's tactics, Martin complained to the ABC about his treatment, and suffered some gleeful media ridicule as a result. Shot for an aborted pilot for ABC TV but replayed, mischievously, on ABC TV's *MediaWatch*, to many of those who saw it the episode seemed like a perfectly appropriate administration of ACA's own medicine.

All of this, of course, is simply water under the bridge. No matter what I might say here, and no matter how much a Ray Martin or a Peter Meakin might claim that this is the commercially naïve criticism of a pc media studies academic, the fact is that the commercial justification for the downmarket trend in current affairs is bankrupted by the simple fact that while it has been in play the numbers watching the programs have plummeted. Further, over the last few years – that is, while this commercial strategy has been in place – the competition at ABC TV, *The 7.30 Report* – starved for funds as it is, and continually fighting off government attempts to take over the editor's role – has been attracting its best ratings since it went national in 1995. (Not to overstate the case, it still finds it difficult to scrape into the top 50 programs of the week, and the improved ratings are a relatively recent development: its drop in audience between 1998 and 1999 was actually worse than *ACA's*.[13]) *The 7.30 Report* has its own problems, as we will see in chapter 5, but it is still doing what it can to maintain the connection between current affairs and the news of the day. Judged against this kind of evidence, one would have to conclude that not only is Australian commercial current affairs television happily feeding in the populist shallows of journalism, but it is (less happily) gradually beaching itself in the ratings.

The future for current affairs television

So, is television current affairs on its last legs? Unless it can revive its importance as a source of information, I would suggest it is. In fact, if all it does (and I stress *all* it does) is to turn news into entertainment then there is little need for it. That would seem to be a view shared by many in the production industry. Media accounts of this situation are littered with comments attributed anonymously to 'industry analysts', or 'network researchers', which would suggest there is a cost to making such observations publicly. When Jana Wendt presented her Andrew Olle lecture in 1997, she bravely attacked the contemporary performance of television journalism, and the responses were both vehement and polarised. There is a lot at stake in this debate in Australia, and much of it is personal. Journalists are not known for their receptiveness to criticism, either – particularly from outside journalism. As Ellen Fanning has noted in another context, '[J]ournalism in Australia is tribal and given the fierce competition between the tribes it is not advisable to show any weakness, to concede any mistakes or to acknowledge any uncertainties'.[14] So, let us use less inflammatory material to develop the case a little further: the following comments are from British media professionals and they come from the ITC study.

At the end of their study, Hargreaves and Thomas present a summary of their conversations with some senior executives in news and current affairs. It makes interesting reading. Richard Sambrook, Director of News for the BBC, acknowledges that the format, as it is currently operated, is pretty much dead: '[T]he days when you could put current affairs in a peak-time schedule and hammock it with entertainment are gone for good', he says (Hargreaves and Thomas, 2002: 97). This may be the lesson that Australian networks are slowly learning, as they vainly try to halt the spiral down-market and retain their audience. Sambrook suggests there is little future in this. Instead, current affairs has to do something significantly different – 'make events out of news', or to create 'landmark programs' such as a vigorously marketed interview with Tony Blair that *Newsnight* spread over three days.

Chris Shaw, Head of Channel 5 News and Current Affairs, admitted that the challenge is how to make current affairs analysis 'grabby and watchable'. He said he was considering running short current affairs films in the 7.30 pm slot, using the timeslot as an experimental one. On the other hand, he rejected the idea that it is uniquely the responsibility of current affairs programs to inform the public. He was irritated by politicians' suggestions that 'everything would be OK if you just put us on telly and get rid of the fluff and allow us to talk about the issues'. Even so, he admitted that 'a bit more original journalism might help'. As he pointed out, the biggest response they receive is when they 'are exposing something new or outrageous' (Hargreaves and Thomas, 2002: 99). All the industry professionals Hargreaves and Thomas interviewed were critical of contemporary coverage of politics and convinced that television needed to find new ways of providing this coverage. 'The idea that three MPs talking about an issue on College Green is good television is just not acceptable' says Steve Anderson, Head of ITV News and Current Affairs, but like all the others he had little to suggest that might be worth doing in its place (100). I am sure we could get similar views, albeit unattributed, from media professionals in Australia.

So what are the options? The ITC report implies that there may be other alternatives that have not been tried. I think we can agree that the downmarket possibilities have been thoroughly explored, and over time have failed to arrest the audience decline. Unfortunately, they have diminished the legitimacy of current affairs as a format: as *Frontline* has so clearly demonstrated, there is declining public confidence in those who work in current affairs, and what goodwill remains is steadily being used up. One possibility the ITC study raises is that of using the format to facilitate more direct public interrogation of political figures – perhaps along the lines of CNN's *Q&A* or the daytime talk show. There is, the authors of the study claim, 'a clear public demand for more occasions in which the public is free to interrogate politicians directly' (Hargreaves and Thomas, 2002: 8). As the authority of television journalists declines, so does their capacity to operate convincingly as surrogates for the audience. One way of dealing with this might be to use television as a means of setting up a direct exchange on political issues between citizens, their elected representatives, and other informed individuals. Hargreaves and Thomas suggest that election campaigns should feature 'a proper series of live party leader debates or, better still, debates followed by an opportunity for members of the public to interrogate party leaders' (8).

Alternatively, the model of the town meeting, where citizens confront newsworthy individuals (perhaps armed with the research performed by journalists), is worth developing as it transfers power from the journalist to the citizen – and does hold the prospect of offering a few surprises. We have seen versions of this in past – think of *Monday Conference* or the various Peter Couchman vehicles – but the presenter/journalist has always held the privileged position. (Indeed, one of the slightly comic effects of Couchman's forums was the inescapable sense that he was always slightly disappointed when he failed to bring, say, right-to-lifers and pro-choice campaigners to some agreement on abortion – suggesting he over-estimated the power of the medium.) A format which empowered the public, and which used the medium to enhance the authority of citizens in their exchanges with the powerful, would be significant. At present the medium is routinely used to build the authority of the journalist or the program, and this is true to varying degrees of even the best examples of current affairs. It could be used to build the power of the public.

Another possibility the ITC study canvassed is a more focused development of the entertainment-oriented chat show, such as *Have I Got News For You?* (the Australian version of this was *Good News Week*). The authors suggest that talk programs aimed at younger segments of the market – in Australia, equivalent programs screening now would be *The Panel* or *Enough Rope* – have the capacity to develop their current affairs potential further by making it a more fundamental, rather than an ancillary, objective of their format.

The most obvious strategy, and one canvassed only last year by the Nine Network, is to reinvest in the provision of investigative journalism – or what these days gets called 'traditional current affairs'. This has been tried from time to time in the Australian market over the last decade or so: notably by the worthy ABC series *Attitude*, the iconoclastic weekly magazine *The Times* (which moved around the schedule, dumping viewers as it went, and so never realised its potential), the Seven Network's *Witness* and most recently by the unconvincing attempts to revive *ACA*'s credibility by employing Paul Barry and Ellen Fanning to perform some longer-term investigative journalism as part of the program's so-called new format. While this last initiative did involve a return to more investigative work rather than just packaging a story, the number of stories Barry and Fanning did – and their impact on the identity of the program – was not substantial. Viewed in the context of the half-hour program, their work ran oddly against the grain of the stories with which they had to rub shoulders, so it would not be surprising if close analysis of the ratings movements during the program revealed viewer discomfort with this. So far, then, in the limited locations where it has occurred, the strategy has not been markedly successful in the commercial or the public sector.

Nonetheless, I maintain my scepticism about the industry wisdom that viewers no longer want to watch politics and social issues generally on television. As I will argue in more detail in the next chapter, this view is not supported by the evidence in the case of *TDT*, nor by *ACA*'s downward slide under its most recent formations, nor by the relative stability of the (admittedly limited) ratings of *Sunday* and *The 7.30 Report*. Nor is it supported by the ratings achieved by *ACA* when it secured an exclusive interview with the newly elected federal Opposition leader, Mark Latham, on Tuesday 9 December, 2003. Matt Price pointed out in *The Australian* that despite the *ACA* producers' 'rule of thumb' that political interviews are 'ratings death', the viewing figures on that night (1.3 million) were significantly higher than those of the previous Tuesday's.[15] Since this rule of thumb has been in place since (at least) 1978 when *TDT* was closed down, maybe it needs to be tested again. Perhaps the coming multi-channel environment, with less dominance for free-to-air, will provide more opportunity for this to happen. We do know that 'serious' current affairs attracts a less fickle audience even if it is not as large as it used to be; it should be possible to build brand loyalty among those who seek such a format but we should not rule out the possibility of more mainstream commercial potential as well.

At this point, though, it is worth asking, 'Why bother about this?' If television current affairs is dying, why not let it fade peacefully away? Why shouldn't we move on to other formats, other kinds of television? There are at least two answers to that which I want to present here, although I will also return to the question for more considered discussion in chapter 7. One answer refers back to the principles that embedded news, information and public affairs in broadcasting regulation in most places: these principles see news and current affairs as one of the benefits that broadcasting licensees can and should offer to the community as a whole in return for their operation of a public resource. Such principles were put in place to enhance the operation of democracy by ensuring the provision of independent information to the citizenry. If those principles were worth defending once, and the need remains today, then the disappearance of the place where they might be enacted is of serious concern.

The second issue has been around for a long time too, and I raised it myself during an earlier discussion of the performance of *ACA* as journalism, which had been provoked by the public furore over the Paxtons' story:

> Journalism has become, in many of its current formations on television today, a means of spuriously legitimating the excessive representational power available to a hybridised genre of entertainment. Journalism ... simply supplies the rhetoric to defend the tactics of [the] program as fundamentally democratic ... (Turner, 1996c: 88)

My point was that current affairs of the *ACA* model seeks to use the alibi of journalism's democratic credentials while delivering a content that most of the time deserves no special protection at all. It is simply a commercial decision to do what they do – even though, when necessary they still have access to the 'last resort claim to the legitimacy of journalism' (89). This, I argued, reduces the possibility of a format more deserving of this kind of legitimation being able to, in the future, establish its credentials.[16] Simply, it devalues the currency.

Television is a conservative industry and big money can hang on its decisions. So, it is worth reminding ourselves that innovative strategies can produce results, sometimes in unexpected ways. The invention of continuous news through cable networks has resulted in a massive increase in the availability of information, and as the ITC report suggests, without compromising the capacity to operate a 'serious news agenda'. As we will see in chapter 4, the development of the late night network news on Australian commercial television in the early 90s came as a response to a series of highly transgressive news formats in which news values seemed to be lampooned: *Graham Kennedy's News Show*, *Robbo's World*, and *Tonight Live*. Paradoxically, these formats actually grew the audience in the timeslot, laying the ground for what has now emerged: a significant extension of the free-to-air news service that is now a standard component of the schedule for all broadcast networks. It is not beyond the Australian industry to believe that a little imagination and innovation might have a similar effect on what now looks like an exhausted format: short form television current affairs. In the next chapter, I want to take us back to where it all began, to the ABC's *This Day Tonight* – as a means of reminding us what innovative formats have done before and could do again, as well as returning to the contemporary debate about whether there is any longer a popular audience for the media's treatment of politics.

NOTES

1   The term 'short form' is used to differentiate between (typically) 30-minute programs composed of a number of items – usually four or five per edition – and 'long form' programs which usually deal with one story developed over 45 to 50 minutes in a single edition.

2   This kind of accusation – that is, about the behaviour of current affairs programs and reporters – constitutes the majority of complaints that FACTS receives.

3   By this I am referring to the tight time limits imposed on the complaints process, the relative inaccessibility of information about progress of complaints, and the fact that effectively the broadcasters are allowed to investigate complaints against themselves. It is only if a complainant really wants to dig in that there is any real prospect of independent evaluation.

4   Interestingly, the study also quotes analysts who describe this as an American commercial trend that is not repeated throughout Europe, for instance, where a strong

public service sector remains even now and where the news diet is defined in significantly different ways (16–17).

5   Significantly, and we shall return to this issue later on, the results for those current affairs programs which dealt primarily with political, social and economic issues – there are fewer of these, of course, and they attract a smaller audience in the first instance – were more stable. In terms of minutes per month, these programs lost only 13 minutes per viewer between 1994 and 2002 (26).

6   Equally instructive is the fact that Jones was a complete dud on TV (notwithstanding his continuing contribution to breakfast TV), Laws was not much better, and Hinch eventually outstayed his welcome as well.

7   For a full examination of how the celebrity industry works, see Turner, 2004.

8   For instance, the proposal to establish a new standard of defence which required published opinion to be 'reasonable' as well as honest has met with considerable criticism which points to the difficulty of objectively establishing what constitutes a 'reasonable' opinion, and to the likelihood that this would discriminate against minority opinions (Morris, 2004: 17).

9   See his autobiographical *Inside Story* (1992).

10   It would be wrong, though, to argue that such stories never came out of commercial programs; an obvious example would be the *60 Minutes* exposure of the Chelmsford hospital cases in the 1980s. My point is that there are now many reasons why such a story might find it harder to make it to air today, and that it would fit less comfortably within the patterns of story selection evident today.

11   For an account of this, see Horrocks, 2004: 55–68.

12   *ACA* presented a series of stories about unemployed youth, focusing on one family – the Paxtons. The audience expressed contempt rather than compassion for this family, and the resulting media coverage demonised them to the point where even the Prime Minister was joining the fray. The issue is dealt with in Turner (1999) and in chapter 3 below.

13   See Figeon & Ellis, 1998. This article reports their ratings slipping 'from a miserable 10.7 average to an almost terminal 8.7' (10).

14   Fanning 2004: 16. It should be noted that this comment is made in the context of discussing Fanning's fascinating documentary about how journalists deal with complex ethical dilemmas in their work, the SBS TV series, *Fine Line*.

15   'Latham's interesting media maul', 11 December, 2003, <http://www.theaustralian.news.com.au/printpage/0,5942,8112114,00.html>.

16   None of this would be a problem if ACA was a game show (Turner, 1996: 89); that it claims to be an ethical participant in the democratic process makes it important that we give it some scrutiny.

CHAPTER TWO

Popularising politics: the case of *This Day Tonight*

The gold standard

Now, time for some history. In local variants of debates about the decline of 'serious' news and current affairs on television, over many years, ABC TV's *This Day Tonight* (*TDT*) has probably become the implicit 'gold standard' against which contemporary performance is measured. While this is usually an assumption, rather than the result of any detailed research or actual comparisons, there are good reasons for such an estimation of the program's importance. *TDT* remains one of the few ABC programs (of any kind, not just news or current affairs) to maintain high audience ratings over a long period. In the first half of its run (1967–73), when it was vigorous, fresh and popular (and also, significantly, national), it rated as high as 25 in Sydney and Melbourne (Horin, 1978: 9). At that time it was what might now be described as a 'water cooler' show – a program that entered into conversation at work and home to the extent that you had to watch it in order to know what your friends were talking about. Even in 1976, towards the end of its run, after the national edition had been broken down into state-based local editions, it was averaging 17 per cent across the nation, and attracting an audience of 1.8 million a night (Milliken, 1977). (*A Current Affair*, remember, attracts around 1.2 million today – this in a national population, and therefore potential audience, that has grown by six million since 1976.)

More significantly for my purposes here, *TDT* also marks the beginning of what we now think of as the standard format for Australian television current affairs. While it was not the first such program (Ten had tried something similar, *Telescope*, which ran from 1965–66 and also featured the first host of *TDT*, Bill Peach, as the presenter), it is usually credited with having first established that the serious investigation of current affairs could be successful and popular television. Furthermore, the program undoubtedly acted as the nursery for a whole generation of Australian current affairs presenters and reporters who would dominate the format from the 1970s right up to the present day. Those who went on to establish major personal reputations since working on *TDT* include (and the fact that there is only one woman in the following list reflects the facts of the situation, not my own gender bias) Michael Willesee, Mike Carlton, Richard Carleton, George Negus, Caroline Jones, Paul Murphy, Peter Luck, Peter Couchman, Andrew Olle, Clive Hale, Stuart Littlemore, Ray Martin, John Penlington, Peter Ross, Gerald Stone, Kerry O'Brien, Tim Bowden and Peter Manning.

Details such as these certainly support the 'gold standard' claim, even though some of those who might repeat that claim today would not be old enough to have ever seen a single episode of *TDT* (it finished in 1978). On the other hand, those who are old enough may well be romanticising, nostalgically remembering the program's highlights rather than accurately recalling its character as an everyday performance of television current affairs. We have already rehearsed in chapter 1 the contemporary concerns about the decline of Australian television current affairs. It would be entirely understandable if such concerns had resulted in some exaggeration of the differences between the journalism of *TDT*, back then, and the journalism of *A Current Affair*, *Today Tonight*, and *The 7.30 Report*, today.

I acknowledge that the choice of topic for this chapter carries with it the danger of implying that *TDT* (and the ABC) is the *only* place where we might find the 'gold standard' for Australian television current affairs journalism. It is important I concede that there are other contenders as well. In particular, to highlight just one, the art of the political interview was probably developed more by Michael Willesee, in the various programs he hosted for three commercial networks over a long period of time, than just about anybody else. In his early vehicles, *A Current Affair* (Channel 9, 1971–3), *The Willesee Show* (Channel 10, 1974), *Willesee* (Channel 7,

1975–6) and *Willesee at 7* (Channel 7, 1976–82), Willesee perfected the strategy of greeting the replies of politicians with a polite, but frankly dis-believing silence – a silence that was embarrassing for interviewees and which they often felt compelled to fill. The early years of Willesee's career were largely spent performing these kinds of interviews and they were reve-latory for their demonstration that one-on-one interviews, without any other content, could be riveting television. Later on, Richard Carleton, Jana Wendt, and Paul Lyneham revealed that they too were especially skilled at the long, filleting, interview. This tradition has largely died, dis-placed – as it was in the running sheet of Willesee's own later programs – by the withdrawal from politics and the embrace of the cosy celebrity inter-view. One could easily spend a chapter examining the history of Willesee's career and his contribution to quality television current affairs. Interestingly, it is very likely that this would deliver a narrative of decline similar to that which I outlined in chapter 1, and which will also shape the account of *TDT* that I want to develop here.

That acknowledged, then, in this chapter, I want to discuss some of what can be learned from revisiting *TDT* – by viewing tapes from the archive in order to assess just what its key textual characteristics were, and by investigating the cultural contexts into which it was broadcast.[1] I con-ducted this research several years ago as part of an inquiry into the history of Australian television news and current affairs. At the outset of the project, I was most interested in the light this archival research would throw on the state of the journalism practised on contemporary Australian television current affairs programs. In this regard, it became clear that *TDT*'s mythic status was indeed warranted: at its best, *TDT* demonstrated the value and appeal of a kind of political journalism that has now almost disappeared from Australian television. However, the research suggests more than this, as it goes beyond the specifics of the practice of television journalism. It also reminds us that there are larger, broader, cultural-political contexts which force us to re-examine our assumptions about the cultural function of television current affairs, and about the kind of audience TDT addressed – as well as, conversely, that which *A Current Affair* or *The 7.30 Report* addresses today.

TDT from the beginning

Viewing sample tapes from the first few months of TDT, I was amazed at how bad it was. At the beginning, there was virtually no attempt to provide a set other than a bunch of nondescript flats to give the presenter a background. The camera framing suggested the producer was unconcerned about where the presenter's face actually was, as long as it was in the frame somewhere. The lack of fill lighting left shadows all over the set and the talent. Camera operation was sometimes appallingly amateurish – with jerky zooms coming in mid-shot and unmotivated reframing all over the place. The lack of an autocue was painfully evident, with awkward pauses as Bill Peach looked for the next bit of the script. Subjects being interviewed were allowed to run on for what feels like minutes on end, with little or no interruption or direction from the interviewer. Politicians and public officials, in particular, clearly felt that they could just sit there and talk at their leisure, without anticipating any interruption. There was, admittedly, a great deal of light and shade in the stories chosen: the deliberately comic set-ups sprinkled through the running order indicated the producers' interest in varying the material. But, at the beginning, the comic items tended to be very heavy handed and sometimes just plain embarrassing; the satiric edge that was eventually to become so much of TDTs character may have been on its way but it clearly hadn't arrived. The list of topics was long, with eight or nine stories in each edition, and the visual treatment was just plain dull. Clearly, at this stage anyway, the ABC was not investing much in the way of resources into this adventure.

As audiences grew and more resources were channelled its way, *TDT* gradually improved over the next three years. The set was progressively styled and upgraded into the 'newsdesk' look still used in such formats today; the lighting improved, and the camera movement was less distracting – although self-indulgent camera work did remain a feature of TDT for a long time. The number of stories used in each edition was reduced, and politics was established as the core territory to be examined. By 1971, the main features of 'the look' of Australian current affairs television were in place: the glamorous and high-tech news desk set, the featured single presenter/interviewer, and the use of background graphics and other visual fill. Bill Peach himself had become something of a television star, as had many of the other reporters (see, for example, the treatment of this in Woodham, 1974). While we might now think of *Sixty Minutes* as the place where reporters first became television personalities in their own right, in fact *TDT* was well ahead of it. Not only were the star reporters such as Peter Luck or Mike Willesee perfectly conscious of their own importance, but they were also by today's standards shamelessly self-promoting in the way they inserted themselves into their stories. It was routine for reporters to use some kind of introductory gimmick or by-play as a point of entry for their stories (in particular, they liked to dress up as a character that was thematically connected to their topic).

Self-confident to a fault, these were no longer the polite and self-effacing interviewers of 1967 and they were regularly accused of rudeness, impertinence and bias. Ironically, while the reporters were busily turning themselves into public figures through the way they investigated and presented their stories (while also making the subjects of their investigations highly visible figures as well), *TDT* itself revealed virtually no interest in what we now think of as celebrity. Members of the entertainment industries did appear from time to time, but the 'celebrities' this program was interested in were in fact the politicians.[2]

On the question of the journalism itself, it would be hard not to look back on this from the perspective of the present without some regrets. Let me take one example: a story from 19 June 1973, an investigation of the New South Wales police who were accused of cynically tolerating the operation of illegal gambling premises in Sydney, and of exploiting the opportunities for corruption this created. This story was introduced by (a young and hirsute) Stuart Littlemore, who provided a news-oriented, filmed account of what his investigation of the issue had produced. His report was supported by filmed location material with a voice-over, as well as some studio material. We then returned to the studio where Bill Peach took up the story, summarising the nature of the challenges presented to government policy on this issue before introducing a studio interview. This pre-recorded interview was conducted by Mike Carlton, and featured a very convincing whistleblower who delivered a stinging critique of police inaction on illegal casinos and the reasons behind it. Carlton did not give this informant a free ride, and his performance was all the more impressive as a result. All of this was interspersed with live crosses to Carlton and Littlemore, who were now in place with an outside broadcast van overlooking one of the most notorious illegal casinos, to provide accounts of activity there. Although the live cross was a bit of a dud (nothing much happened, so Carlton and Littlemore had to wing it for far too long), this was a strong story with a credible informant. It was presented at some length (nine minutes in total), and with a substantial investment of resources (two reporters working on separate angles, as well as two filmed reports and the live cross).

What strikes me most strongly about this example is not only that the program was prepared to invest significant resources into an in-depth investigation of this issue, but that the emphasis was clearly *on the investigation and what it revealed*, rather than on the topic and what could be done to turn it into television entertainment. This may seem only a subtle distinction, but it highlights a significant difference between how stories were chosen for treatment in current affairs television then, and how they are chosen today. *TDT* was oriented towards a process of story selection that was closely connected to the daily news agenda – producers asking what impact they could have on the news agenda of the day, how they could flesh out and background what was already there, or how they could influence the news agenda the following day. It prided itself on its currency and immediacy. Stuart Littlemore claims that *TDT's* commitment to producing what he calls 'the same day story'[3] was why people watched *TDT* – 'that and the studio interviews with politicians and other figures of fun', as he puts it (1996:71). *TDT's* much reduced successor, *The 7.30 Report*, does try to continue that tradition. However, as *Frontline* has taught us, the orientation towards story selection that is dominant within commercial television current affairs today is not like that at all. Instead, the task today is to select topics for their entertainment potential and then decide how the program might construct a story around them.

The result is television current affairs stories that have nothing to do with the news agenda of the day which are prepared in-house and sometimes weeks in advance; they are unlikely to contribute much to the news agenda on the following day – or any other day, for that matter (and we will take up this issue further in chapter 4). These are not news or current affairs stories of social or political importance, deserving close investigation. Rather, they are simply 'product': stories are processed into the news and current affairs format in order to turn them into a recognisable genre of entertainment. At the most elementary, that means they are dressed in public-interest, 'journalistic' discourses, presented by a reporter and organised around the formal principles of objective reporting – two sides to every story, 'challenging' interviews and so on.

The irony is that while *TDT* certainly stuck to the political news agenda of the day, it was also entertaining. Right from the beginning, *TDT* mixed serious with lighter pieces and was perfectly happy to spend a couple of minutes doing something that was, simply, a joke. More importantly, though, the use of humour infected all kinds of stories – from the light-hearted vox pop piece (Peter Luck testing out the social acceptability of the greeting 'G'day, you old bastard' on complete strangers in the street) to the treatment of politics (lampooning New South Wales Premier Robin Askin by having a small choir sing a jolly song with a chorus of 'Run, run, run the bastards over[4]). A satirical mode of reporting was endemic; not only did it produce over-the-top parody and straightforward lampoon from time to time, but it spiced up even the most sober voice-over or introductory set-up. Particular reporters, such as Peter Luck and Stuart Littlemore, were especially prone to this kind of approach and Richard Carleton turned it into a sardonic personal style that he has maintained over several decades of television reporting. It can look more than a little self-indulgent from this distance, but it was certainly a sharp and entertaining way to present comment on stories under investigation. It is not surprising that, while the politicians bewailed the continual use of 'undergraduate' humour from the 'smart-arses' at *TDT*, the public lapped it up.

This attribute of the program is sufficiently central to the format to suggest that the contemporary counterparts to *TDT* are not in fact current affairs programs such as *ACA* or *Today Tonight* (although the John Clarke and Bryan Dawe segment on, initially, *A Current Affair* and later *The 7.30 Report* does carry on the *TDT* tradition). Rather, the approach taken in *TDT* reminds me more of the youth-oriented comedy programs such as *Back Berner*, *Good News Week* or *The Glass House*. Indeed, it has been suggested that *TDT*'s roots lie in an earlier version of this kind of satiric light entertainment, ATN-7's *The Mavis Bramston Show* (1964). Something of a phenomenon in its own right as one of the earliest Australian-made television ratings hits, it was in *Mavis Bramston* that political satire was first successfully attempted on Australian television. The program had grown out of a highly successful local revue tradition at Sydney's Phillip Street Theatre; many of the *Mavis Bramston* cast (Gordon Chater, Noeline Brown and Barry Creyton) had performed in the Phillip

Street Revue. According to Stuart Littlemore, the link with *TDT* is direct. Appearing in a 1992 episode of ABC TV's *Couchman Over Australia*, which reunited some *TDT* alummi to celebrate the 25th anniversary of its first broadcast, Littlemore remarked that the house style of *TDT* was a product of the Phillip Street Revue, not news reporting. It is a sharp observation, which certainly provides some insight into how some of these reporters saw their role. Given such a pedigree, it is not surprising that satiric commentary, not objectivity, was *TDT's* signature. *TDT* alumnus Peter Manning, in the same Couchman program, extended this insight further by contextualising *TDT's* use of satire as the product of a generally anti-establishment cultural ethos he associated with the success of *Oz* magazine, among other things. Indeed, Manning suggested this constituted quite a substantial influence, referring to *TDT* as 'Oz magazine on air'.

TDT's roots in a local satirical and theatrical tradition, then, seem to be well recognised by those who worked on it, while they still insist, as did George Negus in the *Couchman Over Australia* program, that its humour was maintained without trivialising the issues. Some sense of the distinctiveness of this approach might be gained by imagining how 'the smart-arses at *TDT*' might have dealt with contemporary issues such as John Howard's tolerance for lapses in ministerial conduct, or his development of the notion of 'core' and 'non-core' election promises. It would not have been through the wearily respectful interview; more likely, he would have been ridiculed in some satiric skit, or exposed to interrogation by a sneeringly disrespectful Richard Carleton, or met with undisguised incredulity in an interview with Michael Willesee.

The *TDT* audience

Watching the episodes from the early 1970s, you can witness the TDT producers becoming increasingly confident that their mix of satire and politics was working. Indeed, what emerges from reviewing these tapes is an increasingly clear sense of the TDT audience: an audience that was interested in sharply critical and culturally iconoclastic commentary on contemporary politics. This was not a show for the conservative viewer, tuning in to see their attitudes comfortably reinforced for them day after day. The audience you can read off the texts is closest to what we would now think of as a 'cult' audience: what we might now associate, say, with the viewers of *Good News Week*.[5] Yet the ratings are those of a program with broad popular appeal. These days we have become used to thinking of the mass audience as intrinsically conservative and consensual. So it is highly significant that the TDT audience seems to have regarded the controversial nature of the program and its propensity for offending politicians and other members of the establishment as among its most attractive characteristics. This audience was also attracted, I would suggest, by the fact that the program recognised clear cultural and political divisions within Australian society that demanded direct and explicit interrogation. Instead of denying or repressing these divisions – something, one might argue, much of the rest of the culture was doing at the time – TDT enjoyed the process of focusing sharply upon them.

In one edition, a live mock awards program at the end of 1971, some of this audience is briefly visible (it is presented in the 'awards show' format, with the audience at tables and so on) and their affection for the program is palpable. (Again, a contemporary parallel for this is not a current affairs program, but Roy and HG's *Club Buggery*.) Hosted by Bill Peach and Caroline Jones, this program hands out 'the Lefties',[6] TDT's awards to selected objects of their attentions over the year. Examples include the 'Harry Houdini Fugitive of the Year Award': the winner was Michael Matteson, the Australian draft dodger TDT had interviewed live earlier in the year who was still on the run from the Federal Police. The Lefty for 'Keeping a Cool Head in a Crisis' went to Queensland Premier Joh Bjelke-Petersen, who had declared an official state of emergency in Queensland that year when the South African football team arrived to be confronted by massive anti-apartheid demonstrations. The degree of comfortable identification between hosts and audience suggests a closely shared set of attitudes – precisely about the tapes being played before them – which demonstrates how directly the program spoke to and for its audience. What we see reflected back is an interest and enthusiasm for the airing of public issues, and a high level of political information and critical engagement. It is an implied audience, an object of address, which has more or less gone missing from television today.

Even more extraordinary is the audience's support for the controversial nature of the program, something that is repeatedly noted in Bill Peach's memoir and in Stuart Littlemore's boast that on the wall of the *TDT* office there was a league table of current libel claims (Peter Manning was the leader, with $12 million) (Littlemore, 1996: 79–80). *TDT*'s pride in their history of controversy can also be read off the special 1000th edition screened on 30 September 1971. *TDT*, like so much of ABC journalism over the years, had been dogged by accusations of bias throughout its run. It had upset politicians by joining *Four Corners* in refusing to allow public figures to use the ABC's formal commitment to objectivity to silence criticism of government policy. In practice, this convention had required such criticism to be answered directly by government spokespersons on the same program. It meant that government ministers could keep a report off air simply by refusing to comment upon it themselves (see Raymond, 1999, for an account of this issue in the history of *Four Corners*). *Four Corners* had eventually refused to observe the convention, and *TDT* followed suit, cheekily training a camera on an empty chair as a stand-in for the minister in question. The need for politicians to accept their public accountability emerged as a crucial issue for the program, and it was one that audiences clearly welcomed. Nevertheless, as has been the case to a greater or lesser extent throughout the ABC's history, political pressure was direct and effective. Bill Peach's history of the program is riddled with stories of the producers' difficulties in dealing with management's need to placate their political masters. A survey of the newspaper coverage of the period also reveals numerous reports of threats to the program's future, and rumours about management's plans to close it down or draw its teeth (Munster, 1971; Crouch, 1972b; Milliken, 1977).

We are familiar with the embattled and defensive manner in which *The 7.30 Report* has been forced to deal with such issues, often communicating a sense of helplessness, rather than righteousness, in the face of continued political attack from the government of the day. The approach open to *TDT* was evidently very different. Here was a program defending itself from a position of considerable strength – it had a large and loyal audience – and confident enough to go on the attack. The 27 minutes of the 1000th program are devoted to a full-frontal attack on its critics' accusations of bias and rude or aggressive interviewing. Political control over the ABC is dealt with head-on by a tough Bill Peach intro followed by a Gerald Stone interview with Sir Robert Madgwick, then chair of the ABC. A cast of political figures drawn from all parties are asked if they think *TDT* is biased; most say that they have had fair treatment. Importantly, some say it is entitled to take a point of view, and that this is its most significant social function. (Don Chipp, then a member of the federal government, extravagantly suggests that there should be legislation to compel people to watch it!) Where today's ABC must respond to the accusation of 'bias' through an internal review (or even worse, a government-funded report from the Audit Office on ABC impartiality), *TDT* in 1971 vigorously defended its right to a point of view and spurned the refuge of objectivity. Far from defending itself by denying its controversial nature, *TDT* was happy to acknowledge its ability to offend its critics; indeed, the program claimed this capacity as a badge of its significance and value. *The Daily Telegraph's* celebrated vendetta against the program is presented as a comic item, not as a cause for concern. The 1000th edition closes with a montage of short grabs from prominent public figures who support *TDT*. All of this is done with style and humour. In a final round of tongue-in-cheek interviews, asking the elites what they would watch if *TDT* was no longer available, the last comment is reserved for a grinning John Gorton, who says: 'I'd just look around for another comedy program'.

Understanding *TDT's* success involves more than just an analysis of production practices or the texts themselves. The cultural context into which it was broadcast was highly specific, ready to embrace what Michael Willesee described in *TDT's* final episode (1 December 1978) as 'the popularisation of politics' – politics as a sophisticated genre of entertainment for a democratic society. Australian society was on the cusp of repudiating the conservative and domestic ideologies that had sustained it through the 1950s in favour of enlisting in a range of more progressive, internationalising, social movements. When *TDT* started, as Bill Peach explained on the occasion of the program's tenth anniversary (9 April, 1977), Australia had troops in Vietnam and conscription was in place; literature was subject to Commonwealth Government censorship and the phrase 'women's liberation' had not been heard. Other buzz words, such as 'ecology' and 'the environment', were still found only in the dictionary. According to the account given in Bill Peach's introduction, in 1967 Aborigines were not allowed to purchase alcohol and were not counted in the census. The society in place at the end of *TDT''s* run in 1978 was dramatically different and the program had played an important part in making that difference. The treatment of Aborigines was one area where *TDT* itself claimed to have educated Australians and changed attitudes; but it could also claim to have changed the political and social role television played in Australia. As a by-product of its popularisation of politics, TDT had shown how television could enhance the democratic process by demanding that our public officials be accountable to the community.

TDT also demonstrated – perhaps for the first time in Australian history – how decisively television could intervene in the making of a public figure, and how the public figures made by television were going to be different from those who preceded them. The program was explicitly aware of this. In its 10th anniversary episode, TDT reviewed some of the public figures it had 'made' – Don Dunstan, Bob Hawke, Joh Bjelke-Petersen and John Gorton – through a montage of interviews and exchanges. When played back against the mode of representation used in the first episodes in 1967, the difference is extraordinary. The treatment was satiric and irreverent, but it was also highly motivated; the program clearly set out to control the development of the story in hand. A further difference was simply the power television now possessed. This was evident in how the reporters dealt with their subjects. Where initially they had been respectful and compliant, now they demanded direct and appropriate responses. In such an approach, they reflected their confidence in their viewers' support for the principle of public accountability as well as their subjects' awareness of the potential costs of a failure to perform effectively. Both parties had learned what television could do. Fundamental to this was the power of television to augment the public figure's professional persona with new dimensions: the personal, the particular, the mythic or the iconic. It is hard not to conclude that television's novel capacity to deliver a version of the hyper-personal in this way was among the reasons for the program's appeal.

Politics and entertainment

To fully explore the difference between TDT and contemporary current affairs programming would involve a proper cultural history. We would need to examine the differences between an Australian culture that supplied an enthusiastic mass audience to a program offering a diet of politics and undergraduate-type satire, and an Australian culture that now supplies to a cynical and declining audience programs offering a diet of small-time scams, hidden cameras and celebrities. It is not a simple task. Today, as we have seen, political debate is routinely regarded as an audience turn-off, and only the highest-profile political issues make it on to *ACA* or *Sixty Minutes*. Political analysis on television limps along in 30-second grabs on national news reports, or in poorly resourced interviews on *The 7.30 Report* or *The Insiders*. What now seems most remarkable about the *TDT* audience is that they seemed to find politics irresistible – certainly that was true for much of the program's run. Perhaps the novelty of watching politicians called to account for their actions on television may explain some of this appeal. As the novelty wore off, it is possible that this spectacle lost much of its interest. Alternatively, perhaps the power of the spectacle declined as current affairs programs cut their costs, as the talented reporters moved on, and as the televised exchanges became more familiar, more ritualised, more thoroughly integrated into the playing out of the public performance of institutional politics. Certainly, all of these things did happen, but my research on *TDT* has produced many examples of the value of highly qualified reporters working progressively on political stories with the freedom to seek their own information to put before the public. This is a value that has largely been lost to Australian television in the intervening years.

Today, the work of popularising politics has largely been forsaken in favour of a more urgent corporate objective: generating numbers for the current affairs program as the flagship of the network's evening line-up. Most of us would regard this shift as an effect of intensifying commercial pressures, even in the case of the ABC where the need to compete effectively with the commercials in terms of audience ratings (particularly in news and current affairs) remains a relevant consideration. However, the history of *TDT* does challenge the plausibility of this explanation slightly. Dogged by management's fear of the political consequences of its work, *TDT* was subject to a high degree of central control and interference. While one of the ABC's chairs, Sir Robert Madgwick, did present uncompromising support of the program in public (Madgwick, 1969), few other senior figures felt inclined to spring to the program's defence. Indeed, many actively sought to limit its independence. During 1970, there was a protracted public controversy over projected funding cuts, widely supposed to be aimed at closing the program down. At another point, Bill Peach was forbidden to ad lib at all in his intros, and the running order was previewed by senior management staff in time for likely controversies to be snuffed out (Crouch, 1972a; Peach, 1992). Some of the more acerbic (and talented) reporters were pressured out of the program. According to Adele Horin's valedictory report in *The National Times* (19–24 June 1978), among those forced out by a nervous ABC management were Peter Luck, Gerald Stone, Caroline Jones, Peter Manning, Stuart Littlemore, Michael Willesee and Richard Carleton – a 'Who's Who' of Australia's best current affairs talent.

The view reported in 1978 was that this was due to management impatience with the embarrassment caused them by a style of reporting that was often viewed by its victims as aggressive, rude and impertinent.[7] George Negus saw this is as more than an administrative response to some embarrassing moments; rather, it was the result of a deliberate policy to remove the provocation for political pressure by downgrading political reporting at the ABC. As he told Adele Horin at the time, 'the belief at the top was that after three years of Whitlam, people were no longer interested in politics. They talked of doing lighter stories, of trivialising politics. The less politics you do, the less chance you have of getting into trouble' (Horin, 1978: 9).

Conversations I have had with former staffers suggest that the continued campaign against the program by ABC management simply wore them down; by the end, they were simply exhausted from defending their turf. Other accounts differ, however. Stuart Littlemore's memoir reiterates an observation that has had considerable currency: that the angry journalism in which *TDT* specialised, calculated to challenge and change Australian attitudes, lost its force when the Whitlam government was elected. 'Without enemies', he suggests, '*TDT* was lost' (1996: 111) and thus the character of the program was never the same after the 1972 election.[8] Further support for the argument that the audience had lost their taste for political current affairs by the end of *TDT* 's run, comes with the fact that *TDT* was not the only current affairs program which was closed down in 1978. The Nine Network, concerned at what looked like an irreversible slide in its ratings, cut *A Current Affair* and replaced it with nightly episodes of the popular soap opera, *The Sullivans*. This left Nine without a current affairs flagship until 1979, when *Sixty Minutes* arrived.

Whatever the cause (or causes), the changes to the production of *TDT* which came into force progressively from 1975 (the break-up into state editions and eventually the development of the new formats of *Nationwide* and *State of the Nation*) certainly had the effect of downgrading political reporting for *TDT*, if not for the network. Some are in no doubt that this was deliberate. In the *Couchman Over Australia* episode referred to earlier, former *TDT* reporter Paul Murphy explodes at one point: 'They hated it,' he said, referring to management's distaste for *TDT*, and others reinforce the view that management had no real interest in *TDT*'s core business — political current affairs journalism.[9] Bill Peach is slightly more circumspect, but his book (1992) nevertheless provides numerous accounts of the difficulties placed in the program's path by ABC management figures such as Clement Semmler and Talbot Duckmanton, and how these difficulties eventually encouraged Peach to leave the program himself.

The root cause of all this was political pressure. *TDT* was effective in bringing public attention to important issues, and this was not always in the interests of those in government or other positions of power. ABC management was always fielding complaints from such people and rather than defending the right of journalists to investigate the news without fear or favour, they tended to employ what staff board member Tom Molomby famously called 'the pre-emptive buckle': they would accept the criticism without reference to the staff concerned and promise to bring their charges under control. However, even if staff had been willing to help management have a more peaceful life, achieving this was never going to be easy, as Bill Peach points out:

> We were asked to do the impossible and make impartial programs that were stimulating and inoffensive. In practice, we found that it was our offensive programs that stimulated people, and the converse was equally true. (1992: 110)

As for the notion of impartiality, he observed astutely that this 'is not easy to define in a divided society' (110). Nevertheless, the attempts to rein in the program continued, eventually culminating in the vigorous prosecution within the ABC management of what must now be regarded as the convenient view that audiences were now disillusioned with politics, and demanded more lightweight, magazine-style programming. Derek White, the Head of ABC TV Current Affairs in 1978 when the program was closed down, and 'a politically and personally conservative man' (Horin, 1978: 9), was the person blamed at the time. He confirmed to Adele Horin that the conviction that politics was no longer interesting to the ABC's audiences was widely held in the ABC, and that he shared it (1978: 9).

The history of *TDT* raises the possibility that the prime motivation for moving away from its core territory of politics had little to do with audience preferences. Instead, the customary explanation may well be a plausible rationalisation for what was in fact a politically expedient strategy for the national broadcaster – this is certainly the view of some former staffers. Given the control exerted over the ABC's finances by the government of the day, there is always the temptation for government to use this power to influence the nature of the programming produced with those finances. It is a temptation to which governments of both political persuasions have routinely succumbed. Typically, it has been in the reporting of news and current affairs where political interference has been most active, public and insistent; that is, precisely in those areas where there is the greatest conflict of interest. The political pressures upon a genuinely independent investigative current affairs program on the ABC are then enormous, and the history of *TDT* (and of other ABC current affairs programming, then and now) suggests they have a continuing, corrosive effect.

Within the commercial sector, of course, the structural pressures are different, but there is no reason to suppose that hard-hitting political current affairs would necessarily serve commercial interests either. Government support is important to the commercial sector as well, if articulated in different ways: policy debates around the introduction of pay TV, for instance, or of digital television, more recently, have been closely tied up with the commercial consequences of any new policy decision upon the existing networks. Furthermore, as media corporations diversify, and as their level of integration with the business sector as a whole increases, it is not surprising that we have seen an increasing degree of what we might call 'discretion' in dealing with financial and commercial stories. Hence commercial television's focus on small-time conmen rather than the big end of town, despite the last two decades being riddled with high-profile corporate collapses and the normalisation of highly questionable business ethics in major industries, such as banking and insurance. Simply, commercial and political prudence would suggest that a genuinely combative form of investigative current affairs programming was not worth the risk for either sector, so plausible reasons have been found to explain the shifts in format that have taken us away from the core territory developed by *TDT* more than 30 years ago.

The legacy of *TDT*

When we attempt to compare *TDT* with the current affairs programs of today, it is important to accept that there is more involved than just a change in the production of television journalism or some shifts in the templates used to format current affairs television. While these industry-specific narratives of decline are tempting, the differences between what *TDT* did (and who it did it for) and what *ACA* and *The 7.30 Report* do today (and who *they* do it for) are also determined by larger forces. The effects of globalisation, deregulation and commercialisation are not confined to the media industries. Nevertheless, when we look at the specific effects on the media industries, what we discover certainly indicates that there has been a significant change in the function of television current affairs programming in the years between 1967 and today.

A key component has been the political withdrawal from framing media activities within the context of the public interest. This has been an international trend. Once the media were regarded as a component of the democratic infrastructure of the state: they informed, educated and entertained the populace; they provided the platform for the broadcasting of national events; and they also provided the arena within which the public performance of party politics took place. For many years, this public function was seen to be fundamental, even for commercial broadcasters. That is no longer the case, as the deregulatory and privatising momentum built up worldwide over the 1980s has resulted in major changes to the way politicians have viewed media regulation as well as to the way television proprietors have viewed their public responsibilities. As the number of channels available to the various markets around the world increased – in some cases, exponentially (in the EU they increased 560 per cent in the last four years of the twentieth century) – the case for regulation and for any reference to television's former social role (either as an instrument of the democratic state, or as the place where our communities were most visibly imagined) looked increasingly anachronistic. In many markets now the national is a minor influence on the range of television material on offer: that is certainly the case in Canada, for instance. While we are not in this situation in Australia yet, the possibility should cause us some concern. If television did once play a fundamental role within democratic societies, and now it does not, we need to consider whether that role is no longer necessary or if it has simply been abandoned.

Of course, there are other ways of describing this. For some, the decline of what is admittedly a paternalistic, Reithian[10] version of television is an extremely good thing. As a result, it is argued, television now operates through a much more open politics of identity that refuses the elite assumptions behind much state regulation. The insistence on television's educative function, for instance, might be regarded as a middle class imposition against which the adventures of commercial television constitute something of a useful antidote. The media theorist John Hartley (1999) is particularly severe on the class assumptions buried in what I am describing as television's former public service role: he sees it as the expression of a paternalistic suspicion of popular culture and a means of controlling the unruly behaviour of the populace. My difficulty with this kind of line is that it diverts us from examining what might be the actual effects of shifts in the content of news and current affairs – in terms of what is broadcast and what is not. It also sidesteps close examination of the specific national or structural contexts in which the regimes of regulation and control must make their particular political or commercial sense – and in whose specific interests these regimes operate.

I have presented versions of the argument I have been developing here and in chapter 1– that politics can still (*must* still) attract an audience to Australian television current affairs – to conferences and in other public debates. Invariably, it provokes polarised responses. In some cases, the debate is framed as a chicken-and-egg question. That is, we must ask the question: has the coverage of politics on television diminished because audiences are no longer interested, or has it diminished because audiences are no longer interested in the particular way politics is treated on television? Or, to put it another way, is the decline of political current affairs on television a cause or an effect of audience preference?[11]

My response to such questions is complicated. I agree that there has been a significant decline in the public interest in political debate, but I also believe that this has been among the consequences of the character of the debates the public now witnesses – in the media, in government, in the education system. I am encouraged, though, to believe that this is not a permanent condition. Indeed, I was arguing just such a case to a journalism conference on the morning that the Australian Labor Party was making its choice between Mark Latham and Kim Beasley for party leader. Question time after my talk was interrupted by a member of the audience, who had been listening to the radio, calling out the result of this election. The response from the audience did not suggest they had lost their interest in politics!

With all of that said, it still seems to me that, in the Australian context today, we are looking at a cultural shift that is wider and more significant than a redefinition of the public interest in television news and current affairs. It is clear, for instance, that the historical differences between the respective cultural contexts into which these programs are broadcast – between the 1960s and the present – are immeasurably more profound and substantial than the changes within the media professions themselves. *TDT* provides us with a window on to a national community that was politically conservative; at the same time, the public structures available for the prosecution of political change were extremely primitive. *TDT* became an important part of renovating and modernising those structures. It came into being just before the Aboriginal referendum in 1967, and clearly took an active and positive role in airing the issues involved in that referendum. It also joined *Four Corners* in pioneering a new regime of public accountability for public officials – in government and elsewhere. This regime is so well established now that it has spawned a whole new sphere of professional activity to counter its effects – the spin doctors and PR flacks who surround the public officials of today. While regret for such a sphere of activity is often expressed, we might rather congratulate ourselves that such instruments are now necessary at all.

Nevertheless, what has succeeded *TDT* – and not just the programs, I'd suggest, but their cultural context as well – is much more complacent, less critical and less challenging. Journalists wishing to expose affairs they believe should be of political concern to the public have the doubly difficult task of first convincing their editors, and then their audiences, that such affairs matter. As far as we can tell from the evidence of the *TDT* archive, that was not quite such a problem for a society that was on the one hand deeply divided but on the other hand highly attentive to informed discussions of the politics informing their lives. It seems to me that the fading of this latter attribute is the issue that should now be of most concern. James Walter discussed what he called the failure of the Australian political imagination in *Tunnel Vision* (1996) some years ago, framing what 1 am describing as a feature of Australian contemporary culture generally, as well as pointing to what he saw as an alarming contraction in the range of constituencies addressed by Australian politics. Certainly, at the level of popular discourse, one would have to say there is evidence that such trends, whatever their root cause, have had an ultimately repressive effect on the civic imagination and its expression. Ideas, simply, have lost their currency in public debate as they surrender the foreground to simplistic invocations of the economy or the market. Informed discussion is now disingenuously described as 'the chattering of the cultural elites', pilloried for political ends at many levels of society (and usually by those we might describe as political elites). And so what we may learn from this little history of *TDT* is not just about the decline of the process of investigative journalism, or the fading importance of the spectacle of public debate, but a clear sign of the diminution of our commitment to the utility of ideas.

NOTES

1   The ABC archives holds quite a number of *TDT* programs on tape, and they are catalogued in some detail, so that it is possible to trawl through the catalogue for specific stories or topics. For the purposes of this study, my sample was a random selection across the run of the program but it did include some of the landmark programs – the 1000th episode, the 10th anniversary and so on – in order to get a sense of the program's own view of its contribution. Although it is possible to view these at the ABC, I used my research funds to purchase tapes of the programs 1 wished to examine closely. So I gratefully acknowledge the support of the ARC, which funded this project.

2   The current affairs-styled celebrity interview in Australia probably had its origin in Willesee's *A Current Affair* in its initial formation on Channel 7. My guess is that it may well have arisen as a means of exploiting Willesee's reputation as an interviewer and as a point of commercial differentiation from *TDT*.

3   Littlemore defines it this way:

   A 'same day' story was one assigned at the morning meeting (either because the producer wanted it done or, equally often, because the individual reporter had come up with it) which then had to be planned, the contacts made, the location/s reached, film shot, sound recorded, raw

> material brought back for processing and transfer, interviews edited from transcripts, film and sound edited once it had returned from the laboratory, script written and commentary recorded, then that commentary, interviews, sound effects and music all mixed onto a single track for transmission [that night]. (1996: 71)

4   This is a reference to a remark attributed to Premier Askin during the visit of US President Lyndon Johnson in 1966. When the motorcade carrying Askin and his guest was halted by student demonstrators lying across the road, Askin is alleged to have instructed his driver to 'run the bastards over!'

5   By this, I mean an audience that is loyal, well-informed, and more than usually committed to the program. Such an audience will identify strongly with the people on screen, and attribute more importance to the program than is normally ascribed to other television programs – even ones they regularly watch. So, a 'cult' audience will value their choice very highly indeed, and see it as an exceptionally important part of the weekly schedule.

6   Presumably, this name was chosen as an ironic acknowledgment of the program's alleged 'left' bias.

7   George Negus is reputed to have been forced out as the result of what management saw as an aggressive interview with the then Prime Minister, Malcolm Fraser.

8   There were, of course, many enemies remaining at the state level, some of whom (such as Joh Bjelke-Petersen) also exerted a significant influence on national politics, and some of whom (such as NSW Premier Askin) were to provide fodder for current affairs programs for many years to come.

9   Littlemore refers to *TDT* as an 'ever-irritating thorn in the side' of ABC management, and nominates in particular Walter S Hamilton (Head of News and Current Affairs) 'who genuinely detested the program which he simply didn't understand' (1996: 104).

10 This refers back to Lord Reith, one of the founding fathers of British public broadcasting, who took the view that its function was to inform, educate and entertain, pretty much in that order. It is now used as shorthand term for an elite view of public broadcasting that emphasises its educative and civilising functions.

11 Back in the late 1970s, after the demise of *TDT* and the first Nine Network version of *A Current Affair*, a similar question was put by Sandra Hall in a *Bulletin* article announcing the debut of *Sixty Minutes*. Confronting what looked like a decline in the viability of current affairs programs, she quotes a comment suggesting that Malcolm Fraser had made public affairs so dull that nobody was interested any longer (1979: 54–55). *Sixty Minutes* certainly met that challenge successfully.

CHAPTER THREE

From trivial pursuits to predatory practices: 'tabloidisation' and television current affairs[1]

'Tabloid TV' in Australia

In this chapter, I want to return to the present situation in order to look more closely at the content and behaviour which has accompanied the trends referred to in chapter 1, and which provide the point of comparison with *TDT* in chapter 2. As we have seen already, treatments of current affairs' decline have become a staple of contemporary media commentary, especially in newspapers where print journalists will happily cover any perceived failing in television journalism. They have headlines like 'The Big Turn-Off', 'TV's Tawdry Affair', and 'Trivial Pursuits: Why Seven and Nine steered their flagship current affairs shows downmarket',[2] and they all accuse the commercial television networks of competing for their news and current affairs audiences by heading 'downmarket': that is, through their provision of entertainment rather than through their provision of news and information. Instead of focusing on the journalistic quality of their analysis and coverage of news or public affairs, it is said, the networks focused on making stories that could be effectively promoted through the advertising teasers and that were, above all, entertaining. Not only do television's competitors in the print media say this, but it is also raised by those who have worked in the television industry as well – although usually not until after they have resigned. Former reporter

Jeff McMullen's interviews after leaving *Sixty Minutes* are among the more recent occurrences of this.

As I have argued in chapters 1 and 2, there are good reasons for these reports to surface so regularly. Although the justifications for, and the legitimacy of, the market strategies the reports describe might be open to debate, it is not hard to demonstrate that the character of news and current affairs on television has changed and that this has affected more than the treatment of politics. There has been a substantial redefinition of what constitutes news, especially for television current affairs.

The common thread underlying all of this, of course, remains the commercialisation of the news industries; that is, the story could be told through a history of the increasing importance of commercial considerations to the formatting and programming of current affairs over the last couple of decades – something I have already noted as a crucial consideration in the previous chapter, and as a framing contingency in the overview of the industry I presented in chapter 1. The shifts in programming I am interested in here certainly recommended themselves as the appropriate commercial strategies to resist the challenge represented by pay TV and the declining share of the audience enjoyed by broadcast television. And no matter what else we might want to argue, it is undeniable that the dominant influence on the shifts in content and format has been the media industries' own understanding of what constitutes their own best commercial interests. Initially, however, I want to leave commercial issues slightly to one side. Towards the end of this chapter, I want to stress the importance of focusing on what I am calling 'the performance' of television current affairs, and so my first interest here is in discussing the character and content of this programming.

Again, as I have observed already in this book, the prevailing definitions of what counts as news and current affairs in the print and broadcast media have been changing for some time now. There has been a shift away from politics and towards crime, away from the daily news agenda and towards editorially generated items promoted days in advance, away from information-based treatments of social issues and towards entertaining stories on lifestyles or celebrities – and an overwhelming investment in the power of the visual, in the news as an entertaining spectacle. Within the Western news media generally, the pressure to compete has increased as governments adopt more 'market-friendly' regulatory regimes and as the media industries internationalise. The production of news and current affairs has responded to these pressures by re-ordering the principles of selection, composition and representation. The results have been so comprehensively rationalised within the industry that Ray Martin recently defended his practice at *ACA* by pointing to the fact that all *The 7.30 Report* can do is 'the current affairs of the day', thus denying its audience the broader 'public service' that *ACA* delivers (Meade, 2004: 17). At another time, of course, as we have seen in chapter 2, analysis of the current affairs of the day was precisely the 'public service' television current affairs formats were required to provide.

The consequent reconstruction of television news and current affairs' relations with their audiences, with party politics, and with business, has interested more than academics like myself, and it is now among the mythologies which inform popular understandings of how the media functions. Where television news and current affairs professionals might once have been respected as advocates of the public interest, audiences now view the contemporary media's motives and behaviours with more than a little cynicism.[3] Indeed, the comic effect of a small sub-genre of successful 1990s television sitcoms set in television newsrooms (such as the UK's *Drop the Dead Donkey*, Canada's *The Newsroom* and Australia's *Frontline*) depends upon the public awareness of, and liberal concern about, critiques of the contemporary practice of news and current affairs on television.

It has become customary to use the term 'tabloidisation' as a means of labelling the objects of these critiques. As an historical phenomenon, tabloidisation is most definitively located in the British daily newspaper market where it refers to the tabloid-size[4] 'red-tops' such as *The Sun* and *The Mirror*, which focus on crime, celebrity, sex and sport, making maximum use of images, and addressing a populist readership. The use of the term has been extended beyond this original location to refer to a broad range of television formats as well. In the US it has encompassed muckraking current affairs programs such as (the US version of) *A Current Affair*, early 'reality TV' programs such as *Cops*, as well as more recent examples of the genre such as *Temptation Island* and *Big Brother*, and controversy-led daytime talk shows such as *Jerry Springer* and *Ricki Lake*. The category has been developed by those who regard its shared attributes as worrying shifts in the quality and character of contemporary media behaviour. According to these critics – and they can mount a highly persuasive case – tabloidisation has resulted in the media's sacrifice of information for entertainment, of accuracy for sensation, and the cynical employment of tactics which entrap and exploit its subjects (the hidden camera or the reconstruction in current affairs formats, the surprise hostile guest in the talk show).

Not everyone tarred with the brush of the tabloid would accept such criticisms, however. Some proudly accept the label as a means of fore-grounding the iconoclastic and anti-elitist virtues of what they do: among these, the approaches to explicitly exploiting the tabloid can range from the cheeky and responsible to the playful and slightly dangerous (say, from *Judge Judy* to *Ricki Lake*). Others are more duplicitous, disavowing but nonetheless performing tabloidisation. Typically, this might involve a serious program such as *Sixty Minutes*, for example, claiming to occupy the moral high ground of journalism as they expose an issue of 'public interest' (a politician's sex life, for instance) while still tempting the down-market audience with the promise of salacious revelations.

In Australia, tabloid TV has a relatively long history,[5] but its heyday was in the late 1980s and early 1990s when programs such as *Hinch* (1988–1993), *Inside Story* (1992) and *Hard Copy* (1991–1994) were ratings leaders. Such programs explicitly adopted the tabloid newspaper style of headline, incorporating it into the visual presentation of the story in the case of *Hard Copy*, and adopting a classic muckraking populism through such segments as Derryn Hinch's 'Shame File' (which shamelessly lifted stories from the news of the day and exposed the people involved to national vilification). Internationally, at the time, the labels 'tabloid' and 'reality TV' were both in use. American programs such as the 'reality TV' *Cops* appropriated techniques first developed in 'tabloid' current affairs – hidden cameras, hand-held cameras, reporter walk-ins, and so on – and turned them into the standard practice for their own format. Around the world, distinctions between the two categories became blurred as networks strove to invent new formats that nonetheless remained recognisably within current affairs. In Australia, as elsewhere, competition focused on developing an edge in the novelty, promotability, and sensational impact of the stories told rather than in terms of the quality of the analysis or the news values involved.

During this period, as I have noted earlier on, the competition between the Australian commercial networks was exceptionally intense as it responded to the need to service the debts incurred over the ownership upheavals of the 1980s. The flagship current affairs programs were hot property for each of the newly formalised networks[6] and so the competition was fierce at both ends of the market – at the high end, where *Page One* (1988–89) and *Public Eye* (1989) had attempted to situate themselves, and at the lower end, where *Hard Copy* and *Hinch* reigned supreme for a year or two. Ultimately, the industry seems to have decided that the rewards were most likely, and therefore competition was the most fierce, at the bottom end of the market. The long sprint downmarket had begun and the core territory to be contested has more or less remained there ever since. Certainly, the early evening current affairs shows on the commercial networks have observed downmarket or 'tabloid' news values in practice for at least the last decade.

It is important to point out, however, that what we might now describe as tabloid TV is not the same as the more lurid examples from this earlier period, such as *Hard Copy*. True, the diet of crime, celebrities, sex and personal dysfunction that marks many of today's programs also dominated *Hard Copy*; what we see today at 6.30 pm is at least to some extent a consequence of the strategies such programs used successfully for a time. However, unlike the contemporary *ACA* and *Today Tonight*, *Hard Copy* was 'unashamedly tabloid', as its host Gordon Elliot admitted (see Rowe, 1994: 98), investing enthusiastically in stories dealing with violence or sex – or, ideally, incorporating both. Most of its stories came from the USA, and were promoted through *National Enquirer*-styled screamers, such as 'LITTLE WENDY SEX SLAVE!' or 'DIARY OF A STALKER'. Australian stories, David Rowe has suggested in his discussion of the program, were largely incorporated to enable the display of more nudity than was employed in the American material (1994: 102). This was particularly the case where re-enactments were used as a means of exploiting the spectacular, sensational, or salacious potential of the stories.

Far more brazenly than any of its counterparts today, *Hard Copy* used the alibi of news as a means of legitimating something else entirely. Indeed, Rowe's study argues that the format was designed to use the legitimacy of journalism as a means of defending content that could otherwise have run foul of the broadcasting standards regulations of the time. According to Rowe, tabloid TV of this kind 'simulate[d] the conventions of straight "hard"

news in order to legitimise "pornographic" treatments of sexualised violence'
(1994: 99). Consequently, he goes on to suggest that while the scheduling
of such programs in the late evening (*Hard Copy* went to air at 9.30 pm)
effectively sidestepped formal regulatory concerns, there was nevertheless a
public interest case for restricting their exploitation of, in particular, sexual
violence (107). The important point Rowe makes here, and this does remain
relevant for the current and far less confronting formats, is that the public
interest justification for journalistic practice was deployed as a means of
legitimating programs that had little public value at all.

As I have said, it is relatively commonplace for accounts of the contemporary media to refer to the process of tabloidisation, and television news
and current affairs is one of the customary locations of such a process.
However, it tends not to stop there: most often, tabloidisation is used as a
means of gathering together symptoms of other, larger, social and cultural
conditions. Concern about the social and cultural effects of tabloidisation
has become a routine topic for media commentators and pundits of all
political persuasions. One of the reasons for this is that the term has been
applied across such a wide range of cultural locations, without much
regard to consistency in terms of the symptoms or the underlying causes
that are cited. In this next section, then, I want to spend a little time examining the interests and functions the term actually serves, as well as questioning its usefulness as a way of understanding the recent history of the
shifts in the formats of television news and current affairs.

What's wrong with 'tabloidisation'?

In its role as a term of general cultural critique, tabloidisation is custom-
arily framed as a broad-based cultural movement, visible in certain media
forms, which is engendered by the commercialisation of modern life and a
corresponding decline in what are usually called 'traditional values'. While
that might suggest that the concept of tabloidisation expresses a conservative hostility to modernity, and to the media and popular culture as
domains of activity, it must be said that the concept is also employed by
those who would see themselves as political and social progressives, and by
many with a strong professional interest in the media and popular culture.
American cultural and television critic Todd Gitlin, for example, invokes

tabloidisation when he regrets 'the trivialisation of public affairs, the usurpation of public discourse by soap opera, the apparent breakdown of mechanisms for forming a public will and making it effective'. For him, 'trivialisation – infotainment and the like – works against the principled right and left alike. The incoherence of news, the fragmentation of vision, the personalisation of public space militates against all consistent political mobilization' (1997:35).

While he rejects more conventional media critiques such as those mounted in Chomsky and Herman's *Manufacturing Consent* as paranoid and defeatist, Gitlin is in his own way equally gloomy about the progressive potential of the media (indeed of Western civilisation as a whole). We need to admit, he says:

> [T]he possibility that there is a popular will to be distracted and deceived, a will not to know – that is, not to know whatever might jolt one's routines – and that this passion for illusion was integral to Western civilization long before giant corporations became the centres of news and entertainment. (1997: 36)

The highly respected Australian television journalist, Chris Masters, implies something similar in his personal reflections on his experience of working in the commercial sector, as a reporter for Network Ten's *The Public Eye* in the late 1980s:

> My experience in commercial television was an unhappy one. This still disappoints me, because I know the commercial sector is not the Evil Empire. I know the people who work in private and public broadcasting are the same human beings. The problem is that the commercial media is scared about delivering bad news. There is an understandable desire to soothe the public, to convince them that all is well, to be careful about threatening their prejudice and ignorance, and upsetting the status quo. It's hard to convince the public they are right to buy Coca-Cola or Corn Flakes, but wrong about something else. (1992: 237)

This kind of concern is not uncommon within contemporary journalism, and both sets of comments are characteristic in their generalising movement: referring out to larger, commercially driven, trends threatening contemporary culture. That said, it also has to be acknowledged that there is a considerable amount of highly specific evidence and analysis which supports the critique of tabloidisation as it affects the print media and television. Interest in further developing that critique is particularly strong in the 'quality' press, in the universities, and among journalism educators. A typical example is Bob Franklin's book, *Newszak and the News Media* (1998).

Franklin is a British journalism professor, whose book provides a history of the news media in the UK while also mounting an attack on the replacement of news by entertainment which, Franklin argues, has resulted from changes in the news media's structure, regulation, and professional practices. He appropriates Malcolm Muggeridge's neologism 'Newszak' to describe 'news as a product designed and "processed" for a particular market and delivered in increasingly homogeneous "snippets" which make only modest demands on the audience. Newszak is news converted into entertainment' (1998: 5).

While Franklin acknowledges that the media have always had to negotiate between the conflicting imperatives of 'providing information that is essential to citizens in a democracy while at the same time entertaining the public', he argues that the current situation is especially worrying because of the conjuncture of a number of distinctive conditions. The shift in favour of entertainment has never, says Franklin, been so pronounced; further, the effect on investigative journalism in general, and on certain kinds of news (foreign news, parliamentary politics) has been disproportionately negative; its influence has pervaded all media forms to varying degrees; and, finally, it reflects 'an unprecedented congruence of longer-term changes in the financial, organisational and regulatory structures of news media combined with a deregulatory impulse provided by government media policy which will prove resilient to reversal' (6).

Franklin's critique is supported by empirical information which establishes that, given the terms of his argument, there has been a significant shift in the content of news across the media in the UK. For example, comparing the ITV's *News at Ten* in 1990 and 1995, he finds that coverage of international news declined from 43 per cent of the bulletins' content in 1990 to 15 per cent in 1995; sports and entertainment stories increased from 8.5 per cent to 17 per cent; and story length went from an average of 2 minutes 10 seconds to 1 minute 45 seconds. The book argues that research comparing BBC with ITN news bulletins provides evidence of a move 'downmarket'; that is, in all the key indicators (number of news items, duration of each item, range of subject areas and so on) the trend was towards less detail, less background, less politics and more sport, entertainment and consumer items. Franklin notes changes in formats and representational strategies as well, such as the increasing use of the 'live two-way' interview, the intensive cultivation of star presenters, and the reliance on eye-catching visuals. He nominates some broad, structural determinants for the trends he outlines: increased competition, a direct result of government policy on (for instance) cross-media ownership; developments in print and broadcast technologies; and changes in the structure and practice of journalism as a profession, are all implicated.

Once again, these kinds of figures, shifts in formats, and their deter-mining influences, probably would be replicated in the Australian market. If anything, some figures – such as those on story duration – are likely to be even more alarming, as British news bulletins have traditionally used significantly longer and fewer stories than the Australian equivalents. I can attest to the strength of the evidence myself as my own research for a number of previous projects in Australia has revealed similar patterns.[7] That the content and presentation of news in Australia has changed over the last couple of decades seems to me undeniable.

This is not the end of the story, however, because the tabloidisation cri-tique is not driven solely by hard evidence or by a disinterested attempt to accurately map social and media change. Like so many of the arguments about tabloidisation, Franklin's book has a moralistic dimension which occasionally seems to blind him to the cultural values – the specific class-based taste preferences – implicit in some of his judgements. So, when Franklin describes something as 'downmarket', he seems to believe that there are objective indicators for the category upon which everyone would agree. However, as we have seen already, this can be a contentious cate-gory. At the very least, it is saturated with taste implications that make it open to interpretation: what I might describe as 'downmarket', Peter Meakin might defend as 'valid'. At times, then, Franklin's position falls prey to the elitism that academic and journalist Catharine Lumby (1999) has suggested is endemic to such critiques. The opening paragraph of Franklin's book, in fact, offers us an example of 'journalism in decline' which I find highly debatable:

This is how ITN (Independent Television News) anchor John Suchet introduced the filmed report of the funeral of James Bulger for the News at 5.45: 'Hello. The teddy bears he loved so much sat side by side in church today. The day of the funeral of James Bulger. The toys were propped up on a seat that had been made specially for James by his father. It was placed a few inches from James's coffin'. (The accompanying camera shot moves to inside the church and focuses in close-up on the two teddy bears.) It seems unthinkable that this could be the transcript of a genuine news bulletin rather than some grotesque parody of the cynical antics of the fictional journalist Damien Day from the satirical television series *Drop the Dead Donkey*. (Franklin, 1998: 4)

Maybe I have been thoroughly corrupted by the objects of my research, but I don't find this unthinkable at all. Despite Franklin's claim that such exploitation of 'personal tragedy for public spectacle' would not have occurred 'even a decade ago', this does not seem to me significantly different from, say, the media's representation of John F. Kennedy's children during television coverage of his funeral more than 40 years ago. And while it may well be tasteless to some, it does not strike me as an example of any of the practices I would most want to criticise in contemporary journalism. Here, it is hard to avoid the conclusion that Franklin's critique is motivated as much by considerations of taste as by professional principle; he is thus laying himself open to being identified with those whom John Langer attacks as the exponents of a conservative, class- and taste-based, 'lament' about the modern state of the popular media (1998).

There are many problems with the conservative 'lament'. For a start, simply at the empirical level, there are often inaccuracies in the lament's account of contemporary shifts in media content and formats. The fundamental, qualitative, distinction the lament proposes between the approach of the 'serious' media and their tabloid counterparts is actually quite difficult to demonstrate in practice. There is not such a sharp dividing line in terms of content or presentation as critics such as Franklin would like us to believe. In our survey of the treatment of celebrity in the media for the book *Fame Games*, for instance, my co-authors and I found that the trend towards an increasing number of stories on celebrity affected all the media outlets we examined in various ways and to varying degrees (Turner et al., 2000). The shifts in content – from politics to crime, for instance – were evident in all outlets as well. The trends, then, may have varied in their intensity between individual media outlets but they were significant right across the board. I should also point out something else we noticed as part of this study – or rather, that those who worked in mass market women's magazines alerted us to: that there is a certain amount of hypocrisy in some of the measures employed by the 'quality' outlets to avoid looking as if they are as tacky as their 'tabloid' competitors. Hence the regular columns in the Fairfax press, for instance, which report – with amused distaste – selected headline stories from *Who Weekly* or *New Idea* dealing with popular celebrities. Here, the Fairfax papers can have their cake and eat it, too: their can celebrate their elite status in the market by not reporting the stories directly themselves, but still provide their readers with the titillation of the second-hand celebrity content.

The greatest weakness in the tabloidisation agenda, however, lies in its exorbitant comprehensiveness. Catharine Lumby entered this debate in the late 1990s to argue that the public concern about tabloidisation was merely the latest in a series of conservative media panics about contemporary cultural change:

> In the past decade, every conceivable media format, from prime-time news bulletins and current affairs programs to traditional women's magazines seems to have developed a taste for the tabloid. It's a trend which has sparked heated debate in Australia and the United States. Critics across the political spectrum argue the tabloid invasion is responsible for everything from voter apathy to family breakdown. (1997: 117)

As Lumby says, the phenomenon of 'tabloidisation' has become implausibly inclusive; it incorporates lifestyle programming, advice columns in newspapers, afternoon talk shows, viewer video formats, hidden camera journalism, gossip magazines, and much more, into a variety of symptoms for a cultural malaise. Collecting such a heterogeneity of media products under the heading of 'tabloidisation' forces one to respond indiscriminately or, in the case of formats not in any way related to journalism, inappropriately and inaccurately.

Some of these media products are legitimately placed within the history of journalism and are affected by changes in format, address and content which are specific, say, to the tabloid press. Nevertheless, to regard them as the only significant shift to occur within journalism over the current period is simply misleading. In Australia, for instance, while the last two decades have seen the infiltration of tabloid strategies into television news and current affairs, these years have also seen the disappearance of the vast majority of metropolitan tabloid newspapers and the recognition that the 'quality' end of the newspaper market contains the best prospects for sales growth. Further, over the same period, Australian commercial television networks have significantly increased their daily news coverage, with Nine and Ten (Seven did this for some years, too) running a late news bulletin of up to 30 minutes which has substantially increased the number of sets in use in the timeslot, while Seven and Nine have increased investment in their early morning news programs.

Some pet targets of the lament have no place in the argument at all; they simply belong to a list of those things the complainant finds offensive about contemporary popular culture. It doesn't much help our understanding of, say, Oprah to see it as representative of the cult of the personality and the trivialisation of news values held to be consequences of tabloidisation. It is more productive to see Oprah's appeal in the way feminism has tended to do, as a program which accesses modes of expression identified with sections of the community hitherto virtually unrepresented in the media – except as victims in the news. Oprah's success probably needs to be tied to a larger, different, cultural shift in the content and function of television visible in network prime time through formats which deal with personal relationships, confessional talk, lifestyles, celebrities and entertainment. As the pattern of programming reveals the effects of this shift towards the private, the domestic and the feminine, it is clear that television has entered a new phase in its participation in community debates and in the formation of personal and cultural identities.

It is this aspect which has mobilised most criticism of the tabloidisation argument. Lumby suggested that criticisms such as those in Franklin's book were aimed at protecting traditional definitions of what matters in 'public affairs' – business, parliamentary politics, economics, the law and so on – against new, competing agendas. It was time, she argued, that the traditional definitions of what counted as news were challenged by other considerations: the private, the domestic – above all, by the feminine. For Lumby and for many others working on new trends in television, tabloid news and the afternoon chat shows such as *Oprah* and *Ricki Lake* stood as positive markers of an expansion in the range of issues, political positions, and voices becoming audible through the media:

> The tabloid trend has put 'private' issues on the nightly televisual map, from domestic violence and child abuse, to relationships, addiction, eating disorders, parenting problems and sexuality. It blurs the boundaries between women's stuff and traditional public policy matters. And by juxtaposing the usual serious news with the tabloid – putting the public health problem of drug abuse up against personal battles with addiction, for instance – it connects the public and private spheres in an intuitive way that feminists have long agitated for at the public policy level. (Lumby, 1997: 117–18)

Since then a substantial body of writing about the US talk shows[8] has supported Lumby's argument, in principle if not always in practice, suggesting that they offer a new form of subjectivity and agency for otherwise silenced sections of the community – such as women, racial minorities, and the working class. Lumby's second book, *Gotcha! Life in a Tabloid World* (1999) took the argument further, celebrating 'the tabloid' as the sign of a more democratic and accessible media and calling for a more dispassionate analysis of contemporary media trends that assesses it in its own terms – rather than against outdated and elitist standards of media performance. Similarly, the American writer, Jane Shattuc, who has researched the growth of American television talk shows, suggests that the media panic about tabloidisation, in relation to these programs, is at least partly located in middle-class anxieties about the disintegration of their power to police the standards of popular behaviour (1998: 224).[9]

Let me sum this up, then, so that we can move on. There are enough problems, in my view, to make the category of tabloidisation of limited use in helping us investigate the content and performance of the contemporary media. Specifically, the category of tabloidisation is now too baggy, imprecise and value-laden to be of any use to me in attempting to understand the appeal and cultural function of contemporary news and current affairs. In particular, and this is where I want to go next, it doesn't help us understand one of the most common and worrying aspects of the contemporary performance of television journalism. This is what I would describe as the predatory dimension of current newsgathering tactics: the relentless intrusiveness of the paparazzi; the bullying, foot-in-the-door reporter who uses media exposure as a weapon and as a genre of personal performance; the lynch-mob mentality of so-called 'attack journalism'; or the sleazy self-righteousness of the hidden camera stories. I think we are justified in expressing concern about these areas, where the issues are those of the abuse of media power rather than of taste or shifting news values.

What I am describing as the *performance of journalism* – what journalists actually do in the media, at whose expense, and in whose interests – should receive more scrutiny than it does at present. To some extent, the tabloidisation critique diverts us from this, as if by describing something as 'tabloid' we have done enough; or, as if the sweeping comprehensiveness of the critique relieves us of the responsibility of examining what is actually wrong with particular instances. Most importantly, though, the behaviour I am concerned about is not limited to a particular market positioning – 'downmarket' or otherwise. Rather, it is a widespread mode of operation that is the consequence of the media's evident confidence in its own power: in this case, in the program's power to control representation and its readiness to exercise that power in its own interests. Here, the commercial determinants reappear, because it is the commercial interests of the program that matter most and which motivate the kinds of performances I have in mind. These performances do not serve our society well. There are many examples to choose from, and they proliferate daily but, by way of a familiar illustration, let me remind you of a notorious example from *A Current Affair*.

Predatory practice: the case of the Paxtons

Many readers will remember the furore that arose when, in March 1996, *A Current Affair* ran what started out as a story on the destructive effects of long-term youth unemployment. In the initial, relatively sympathetic, piece three unemployed Melbourne teenagers and their mother, the Paxton family, were interviewed in their home; one of the three teenagers was shown, stagily, getting out of bed at 11 in the morning, a victim of the apathy produced by the lack of job prospects. A follow-up story set out to 'do something for these kids'. They were flown to a tourist resort in North Queensland, 3000 km from Melbourne. Shane and Mark were offered labouring jobs while their sister, Bindy, was offered a job as a waitress in the resort restaurant. There was a hitch, though. The resort had a policy which required their employees to cut their hair short, something the boys refused to do. Stuck with the prospect of moving there alone to work as a waitress, Bindy (aged 16 at the time) mumbled something about disliking the colour of the uniform and declined her offer too. Dumping the heart-warming 'we'll fix it' story without missing a beat, ACA turned it into an indignant 'teenage dole-bludgers' story. The three were shown flying into the Whitsunday Islands, riding on a catamaran, taking in the beach, and then scandalising the parents of Australia by turning down the job offer of a lifetime.

All hell broke loose. The network's phones ran so hot with outrage that ACA was able to cover the public reaction to their story on the following night. The Paxtons' neighbours were offered the chance to fire off some vox pop vitriol, the Premier of the State of Victoria deplored them, even the Prime Minister (being interviewed on the same show to talk about his newly elected government) was happy to agree that the Paxtons' actions were 'totally unacceptable'. The ratings went through the roof, so it didn't stop there. ACA demonised the family for six consecutive nights. Only in one story (of the total of eight) did ACA provide air time to anybody pre-pared to defend the family: this was Chris Puplick from the Anti-Discrimination Commission who pointed out, to no effect, that it was in fact illegal to require anyone to cut their hair in order to gain employment unless it was an issue of health or safety. Eventually the family realised they were never going to get their side of the story heard and refused any further interviews. 'We don't want to be in it any more', Mrs Paxton said, in a choice of phrase that indicates something about how she was encouraged to be 'in it' in the first place.

Elsewhere in the media, some were smelling a rat. The family main-tained that they had been set up and that ACA knew they would refuse jobs which required cutting their hair. Inquiries at the resort indicated that a barber's appointment had been booked for the boys before they arrived.

Media commentators Phillip Adams and Stuart Littlemore attacked the program, its presenter (Ray Martin) and the reporter (Mike Munro), for manipulating vulnerable teenagers and cynically exploiting the results. Littlemore, hosting the ABC's *MediaWatch*, screened out-takes of the original interview which showed Shane Paxton telling Mike Munro that he would not cut his hair to get a job. It was also suggested that the whole affair was a publicity stunt for the resort, which was in financial trouble (it was placed in receivership six months later). In his column in the national daily, *The Australian*, Phillip Adams suggested just where he would like to stick Ray Martin's recent Gold Logie award. A talkback radio announcer in Melbourne came out in support of Shane Paxton, attacked *ACA* and the Nine Network (a key advertiser with his station) and promptly lost his job.

How did the Paxtons benefit from their decision to allow the leading national current affairs program to represent their point of view on the difficulties they experienced in dealing with long-term unemployment? They were spat upon in the street, pilloried in the press, and received death threats. In a crowning irony, the dole office cut off their unemployment payments because they had refused a legitimate offer of work. Eventually, inevitably, Shane's notoriety landed him a job in the media – as a youth affairs spokesperson for an *ACA* competitor – but the novelty soon wore off for both parties to the arrangement. Inevitably, too, the November 1996 issue of *Australian Playboy* featured a topless pictorial of Bindy Paxton alongside a defiant interview expressing her anger and resentment at *ACA*'s treatment.

The producers of this story probably started out genuinely intending to help the audience understand the corrosive effect of unemployment upon young people. This positive story was reframed in response to the audience reaction: the nastier the treatment got, the higher soared the ratings. It would not be easy for commercial current affairs producers to resist the momentum this built up, and in this case it seems they made little effort to do so. In a spectacularly irresponsible series of segments, the program shamelessly pursued the ratings despite the fact that they were hugely victimising a family who were already at risk, and who were unable effectively to defend themselves.

This is a well-known example but only one among many – and I should acknowledge that they are not only found on *ACA* or the Nine Network. There are plenty of instances where ordinary people find themselves the innocent victims of media power, and where the news media do whatever they want – because they can. British tourist, Joanne Lees, found herself in that situation in 2004, as the centre of media interest when the committal hearing of the man charged with the murder of her boyfriend, Peter Falconio, commenced in Darwin. Witnessing her appearance in the same court where years before Lindy Chamberlain had attempted to change the mass-mediated public perception that she had murdered her baby, the media invited speculation that Lees herself was in fact the guilty party. In such situations, television current affairs is far from the only culprit, but it is a highly influential one. Furthermore, over its recent history in Australia – from the arrogant buffoonery of Hinch's 'Shame File' to the Sunday program's mischievous airing of Mark Latham's former wife's domestic resentments – Australian television current affairs has consistently produced examples of the power of the media having been employed irresponsibly.

There are many questions you could ask about such stories. Why did experienced professional journalists participate in the Paxtons' lynching? If it was because their producers insisted they did so to further increase the ratings,[10] then maybe we should ask how media producers have come to believe they have the right to intervene in ordinary people's lives in such a way – simply to produce a commercial result? Nick Couldry has argued that the media has convinced us that they are the 'social centre' of our society (2003: 143). There are 'media people' and there are ordinary people: to really matter, we must become 'media people'. He uses this to explain why people agree to allow the media into their lives – and the point would apply to the Paxtons as much as to the contestants on Big Brother, which is Couldry's initial point of reference – as a form of validation, a point of access to the social centre.[11] Maybe it also works the other way. Perhaps, those who think of themselves as belonging to the category of 'media people' develop a disproportionate sense of their own social centrality. As a result, normal social and ethical constraints lose some of their cogency and any socially responsible criticism of their actions just comes across as a failure to understand the importance of what they do. This must be a delusionary world to inhabit.

The more difficult question, perhaps, is why so many people chose to watch the Paxtons' humiliation, avidly, night after night. This something that my field of cultural studies – focused as so much of it is upon the consumption of popular culture – should be able to help us with. But it hasn't done much in this direction so far, and the reasons aren't hard to find. Cultural studies learnt during the 1970s that it was not good enough to dismiss popular audiences as 'cultural dopes', and so perhaps we became reluctant to look at examples of media performance and programming that tempted us towards such a judgment. In many cases, this may have accorded with our personal preferences and enabled us to explore, along the way, our enthusiasms for certain popular cultural forms. As a result, cultural studies knows a lot about the appeal of soap opera, game shows, drama series, and music video, but there are still very few elaborated explanations for the success of reactionary and/or populist media products: newspapers like *The Sun* in the UK, men's magazines like *Ralph*, the 'shock-jocks' on talkback radio in the US and Australia, or the bottom end of the reality-TV phenomenon which includes *Temptation Island* or *Something About Miriam*. By and large, while noting their significance (and, I admit, with some notable exceptions), cultural studies has preferred not to deal with these media products in any detail and has taken their offensiveness, more or less, as read.

The word 'offensiveness' is a crucial one here. Importantly, it is worth acknowledging that the 'offensiveness' of such media products is, in a sense, deliberate. To criticise them for their regressive cultural politics or standards of taste is to miss the point. Jane Shattuc, in the discussion of US talk shows referred to earlier, describes most media criticism of these popular formats as an attempt to bully the popular audience into adopting more middle-class standards of taste. Yet, she points out, these are standards which denigrate, repress and subordinate those tastes or 'regimes of value' identified with less powerful sections of the community. The media producers are onto this, too; that is why they accuse their media critics of being out of touch with what the audience wants. Those whose favourite programs are among the targets of such critiques are aware of the class basis for the criticism; hence the popular audience's frequent adoption of a mode of consumption which happily offends elite and middle-class tastes. As Andrew Ross put it, the 'offensiveness' of much popular culture is actually designed as a 'deliberate affront to elite standards and to the intellectuals who defend them' (1989: 231).

So far, so good, but what also continues to be puzzling about the audience interest in such popular media texts as the Paxtons' stories is their victimising of those who are already marginalised or dispossessed. These are people, one would think, with whom the audience might sympathise. But they don't; most often, the audiences rejoice in the victim's humiliation. Many years ago, the sociologist Ralph Milliband argued that the resentment produced by class subordination produces a search for victims – in the media and elsewhere – to reduce the sense of oppression. He called this the process of 'de-subordination'. Desubordination means 'that people who find themselves in subordinate positions and notably the people who work in factories, mines, offices, shops, schools, hospitals and so on do what they can to mitigate, resist and transform the conditions of their subordination' (Milliband, 1978: 402). One of the ways of doing this is to locate others who can, in turn, be regarded as more subordinated or oppressed than they are themselves. Television current affairs programs provide an endless array of contenders for this process. Jim McGuigan, one of the few to look carefully at tabloidism in the newspaper industry, has come up with a similar idea by proposing a connection between the scandalous popular pleasures available in The Sun newspaper (UK) and a resentful politics of the dispossessed among its core readership (1992: 184). According to such an account, a corrosive populism – expressed in these media forms as a deliberate affront to decorum and taste – could be understood as the product of a vengeful and destructive version of de-subordination. A grim picture, one that probably accords a little too closely with elite diagnoses of the mass media audience.

To stand back from it somewhat, this 'corrosive populism' may simply be the negative to the positive accounts presented by Shattuc and Lumby; that is, both versions have significant explanatory power but neither, on its own, can present us with the full spectrum of the competing political potentials of the popular media. In fact, I think it is genuinely difficult to understand why a popular audience would tune in to watch one of their own vilified, gratuitously, on a national current affairs program. But I don't think we have to solve that problem in order to be concerned about the way the program concerned milked that interest, nor about the effects of the media's behaviour on those involved.

So, on the one hand, I am saying that we need to be aware of the class-based, elitist, and gendered implications of much of the standard lament for the decline of journalism that I have summarised under the label of 'tabloidisation'. On the other hand, that doesn't mean we should complacently accept whatever television throws up for us; rather, we need to continually subject the performance of news and current affairs to critical scrutiny in order to evaluate what it actually does as an ethical, social and political practice – not just as entertainment.

It would be wrong, then, to classify mine as simply another voice added to the chorus of criticism of tabloidisation. Rather, I am more concerned with what television journalism actually does, who it does it to, and in whose interests. Such an account of this domain of media performance has the potential to radically change our understandings of television journalism. For a start, as we have seen, it disconnects journalism from the more positive versions of its social function – the ethically driven, journalism-as-a-pillar-of-democracy definition implied by Franklin's approach, for instance. Ironically and regrettably, it suggests that this traditional view of journalism has also been used quite cynically: as a means of legitimating the worst of the predatory practices currently employed. Certainly in the case of television, I think there is evidence that often, if not routinely, the 'information-democratic' definition of the social function of journalism is appropriated to mask the commercial motives of those dealing with the lives of the public and to plausibly defend journalists' right to use whatever they can as they see fit. I do not see this as a consequence of tabloidisation but rather of the failure to fully recognise or, alternatively, of the capacity to obscure, the implications of journalism's institutional reconciliation with its commercial function as a form of entertainment.

NOTES

1   This chapter draws upon material which was published in slightly different form in my article, 'Tabloidisation, Journalism and the Possibility of Critique', *International Journal of Cultural Studies*, 2:1, 1999: 59–76.

2   Casimir,1998: 4–5; Meade, 1999: 2; Meade, 2002: 4–5.

3   See MacLean, 2004c.

4   The less controversial way of using this term is to distinguish between the larger 'broadsheet' format of newspapers (such as, in the Australian market, *The Australian*) and the smaller 'tabloid' format (such as, in the Australian market, *The Herald-Sun*). The tabloid format was connected to the commuter market using public transport, and that is one of the reasons for it having a working-class connection.

5   We might even date it back to the beginning of *Sixty Minutes* in 1979 as the place where the focus upon the star reporter and the star informant injected some showbiz glamour into the format.

6   At the end of the 1980s, a series of ownership changes and policy shifts resulted in

the formalising of the national television networks; hitherto, they had been a mixture of formal and informal alliances as the media ownership regulations prohibited the three major networks from owning a channel in each capital city. Once this rule was relaxed, Australia had its big three commercial networks and competition became a truly national affair.

7   See Turner et al., 2000, and Turner, 1996a. I am thinking here of trends such as the increased treatment of sport and celebrity, the replacement of politics by crime as the dominant category of story, and so on.

8   In particular, Jane Shattuc's book *The Talking Cure: TV talk shows and women*, (1997).

9   While she is certainly alert to the highly contradictory politics of such shows and of their likely relation to their audiences, Shattuc ultimately defends the talk shows as an 'important venue for average people to debate social issues that affect their everyday lives', and regards much of the media concern about their outrageousness as evidence of the difficulty experienced by the American middle class when forced to deal with the 'impolite and impolitic behaviour of its underclass' (1998: 222).

10   That would be my preferred explanation in the light of public and other comments made by insiders at the time.

11   A more developed discussion of this can be found in my *Understanding Celebrity*, 2004, chapter 3.

CHAPTER FOUR

Shifting genres: the trade between news and entertainment

Genre-blending

I want to approach the 'trivial pursuits' of chapter 3 from another perspective, viewing it as the product of a complicated trade between the genres of news and entertainment that could be incorporated into a more positive account of some of the histories – and by implication the possible futures – of current affairs in Australia. As we have seen already, the standard alibi for the shifts in news and current affairs I have been discussing in this book is that they have been necessitated by the audience's demand for news and current affairs programming that is entertaining. Implicitly, 'news' and 'entertainment' are set up as opposites. In order to make the boring substance of news palatable to a mass audience, you have to make it entertaining; if that means that some of the 'news' content of news has to be sacrificed, so be it. The discussion of tabloidisation presented in the previous chapter probably reinforces the status of such an opposition because it foregrounded the way that commercial considerations have influenced the development of contemporary formations of news and current affairs. This needs some qualification now, and my point of view requires some further explanation as I am not simply arguing against a more populist, entertaining form of programming. Indeed, I want to discuss certain points where innovative and challenging approaches to news and current affairs have been tried in Australia, while also attempting to refine the diagnosis of what precisely is missing from the contemporary situation – something which a loaded term like tabloidisation, or a fixed opposition between news and entertainment, won't necessarily assist us to accomplish.

While the late 1980s–early 1990s may well have been the starting line for the race downmarket, they were also years of an especially rich period of Australian television history, when innovative program ideas (good and bad, successful and unsuccessful) proliferated. If we were to focus on some of these developments, which might tell a different story to that out-lined in the previous chapter, we might conclude that the trade between the genres of news and entertainment – between news and game shows, talk shows, and even variety formats like the 'Tonight' show – does not have to result in the trivialisation of serious news or in the predatory commer-cial practices discussed in chapter 3. The histories I will deal with in this chapter provide examples of genre-blending where the outcomes have been extremely varied, and at times entirely consonant with the values underpinning traditional conceptions of news and current affairs.

A way to start is to acknowledge the simple fact that the trade between news and entertainment formats is two-way: that news and current affairs have infiltrated entertainment formats as well as the other way around. The distinction between the current affairs interview and the talk-show inter-view, for instance, has been blurred for quite some time. The celebrity interview is probably the place where this blurring first occurred and where it has now become more or less institutionalised; it has become a staple component of the current affairs as well as the talk-show formats. Most talk shows, of course, do not only deal in celebrity interviews. The UK's Michael Parkinson is an exception, since he largely limits his subjects to celebrities from the world of show business, but the leading US network talk shows do not. David Letterman and Jay Leno regularly interview politi-cians and other people in the news, while Oprah Winfrey has an explicit set of social and political interests which she prosecutes through interviews with advocates, experts and celebrities as well as through vox pops from the audience. Such shows, then, have developed a hybrid talk and current affairs format.

In Australia today, an example of the hybrid talk /current affairs show is Andrew Denton's Enough Rope. Highly intelligent and an effective inter-viewer, Denton is not a journalist but an entertainer. The apparent 'softness' of *Enough Rope*'s interview format may well attract guests who really don't want to expose themselves to a current affairs journalist; when Bill Clinton was in Australia to launch his autobiography in 2004 his only extended interview was with Denton. As the title implies, though, this can be a little misleading and guests can reveal more than they expect. On the face of it a slightly idiosyncratic take on the 'Tonight'-styled variety show, *Enough Rope* has nevertheless broken news stories; this happened after Denton's interviews with Rene Rivkin and with John Laws, for example. *The Panel* is a hybrid as well, consisting primarily of talk about current affairs interspersed with interviews with figures in the news – mainly from show business or sport, but not exclusively. Even though some members of the regular cast of *The Panel* are highly opinionated and keen to display their views, this never turns the interviews into the challenging interrogation one would expect from a journalist (or, indeed, from Andrew Denton). As a result, *The Panel* does not break news; it simply provides the opportunity for a relatively articulate form of Generation X *vox pop*. Significantly, the regular cast on *The Panel* generates entertaining conversation rather than investigation or analysis; they don't have to be well informed (that's what the guests are there for) but they do have to be fun. In the case of such regular members of the team as Rob Sitch, Tom Gleisner and Santo Cilauro, their track records have already demonstrated their capacity to do that: the popular success of their feature film *The Castle* is probably the key element here. However, their credibility as commentators on the news – to the extent they have any – also derives from their entertainment backgrounds because so much of their earlier work occurred in socially and politically engaged television satiric comedy (*The D-Generation*, *Frontline* and so on).

Satiric comedy programs, of course, are traditional locations for political comment, as we have seen already in the discussion of TDT, and the present inheritors of that tradition are the ABC's *Back Berner* or *The Glasshouse*. But there are other genres that have been infiltrated by news and current affairs content as well. *Good News Week* (ABC, and then Ten) was a satiric game show in the late 1990s, modeled on the British *Have I Got News For You*, which was based on news reports and current affairs knowledge. Occasionally, too, high-profile politicians (examples included Amanda Vanstone, Gareth Evans and Natasha Stott-Despoja) have sat on their panels and taken part in the program. The ABC's *CNNNN* and *The*

Chaser are both modeled explicitly on current news formats, wickedly satirising both the content and the representational conventions of the news on television.

It is the comparatively youthful demographics of such relatively niche-marketed[1] and genre-blending (some might call them 'cult') programs that gives point to the research referred to earlier which indicated that young people prefer to derive their news and current affairs information from entertainment formats rather than from news and current affairs programs. It reinforces the hunch I outlined in chapter 2: that the problem with political stories in television news and current affairs programming has a lot to do with the way they are currently formatted and pitched. Crucially, in all the examples I have mentioned, news and current affairs material is dealt with by presenters who are explicitly not journalists. They don't pretend to be, either – unlike a talkback radio host such as Alan Jones, who strenuously appropriates that kind of authority to shore up the credibility of his personal opinions. These presenters are content to come across as amateurs. As a result, they do not work at generating the authoritative voice that has become the professional mode of address for current affairs reporters and presenters over the last couple of decades. Instead, their programs have employed a 'post-journalism' approach to covering social and political issues: that is, they are defined by their separation from – perhaps even by their distaste for – contemporary news and current affairs journalism conventions and practices (and we will return to this idea later on in the chapter).

Notwithstanding that observation, it is fair to argue that this trend still constitutes an expansion of the content and purchase of news and current affairs, even though it might be represented in different ways. News and current affairs have infiltrated entertainment formats, turning them into alternative locations for information, analysis, and even, sometimes, debate. In what follows, I want to develop this possibility by looking at the histories of some programming innovations that seem to me to have blended the genres in interesting, original, and entertaining ways. Importantly, they remind us that even when Australian television news and current affairs has redefined itself most aggressively around the imperatives of the ratings and entertainment, there have been developments from which the defenders of news might still draw quite positive conclusions. In both of the following cases, a slight whiff of originality in the production design generated a whole cycle of programming innovation in the presentation of news and current affairs: consequently, they teach us a lesson about the potential of the medium which is still useful. I want to look at two developments: the invention of the late night news audience, and the attempt to recover the youth audience.

Robbo's world, Kennedy's audience, and Jennifer Keyte's legs[2]

My starting point is the origin of what is now the late night news slot – the half hour bulletin presented at roughly 10.30 pm over most of the 1990s by all three commercial networks and the ABC. Seven dropped its bulletin some years ago, but there were reports in 2004 that it was planning to revive a late night news service; that would return us to the situation where all free-to-air networks provide a late night bulletin. While we might be used to this component of the television schedule now, it was only towards the end of the 1980s that serious competition between the national networks for a late night news audience first developed. Until then, the 10.30 pm slot had been a dead spot in the schedule; typically, it was the time when Australia went to bed (except in Queensland, when it was 9.30!). The competition that developed at the end of the 1980s turned that around, and increased the number of sets in use in the timeslot (Williams, 1996). Interestingly, this is unlikely to have been the result of an interest exclusively in news. In a striking parallel to the trends I noted above in relation to the hybrid talk/current affairs shows of today, the development of the late night timeslot for news during this period originated in a ratings duel between programs hosted by Clive Robertson and Graham Kennedy, neither of whom were journalists and neither of whom showed any respect for the news they presented. In fact, both of them were deliberately subversive of the discourses and the power of television news, and were happy to attack its credibility as a means of getting a laugh. When their competition had run its course, however, what was left behind was a more or less standard edition of the network news.

Clive Robertson had been something of a cult figure as a highly idiosyncratic ABC breakfast radio host before he began reading the late night news on Channel 7 in Sydney in 1986. *Newsworld*, as the program was called, was networked nationally in April 1987, building up its ratings in most markets (Melbourne was resistant) over the next two years. Such was his success that the graveyard spot of 10.30 pm became the location for a fierce ratings contest for the first time, with Robertson provoking competition from Graham Kennedy's *News Show* (later to become *Graham Kennedy Coast to Coast*) on the Nine Network. While Robertson eventually lost this battle, Kennedy's subsequent departure from *Coast to Coast* allowed Robertson to move to Channel 9 to present in its place *The World Tonight with Clive Robertson*. The ratings duel revealed a commercial opportunity for the timeslot, encouraging the Seven Network to develop Steve Vizard's talk show, *Tonight Live*, to compete against Kennedy, first, and then, Robertson. Vizard eventually prevailed. In August 1992, *The World Tonight* folded, Clive Robertson was sacked and his show replaced by *Nightline* which was hosted from then until 2003 in a more conventional manner by the much less idiosyncratic Jim Waley.

Clive Robertson's Newsworld was a radical departure from conventional news broadcasts on Australian television (see Wilson 1994). Robertson was the antithesis of the traditional news reader. He was opinionated, lugubrious, insulting, and often appeared just plain depressed. He made faces every time he had to mention Ronald Reagan or Bob Hawke, and on occasion would simply refuse to read certain reports – such as the results of races in the America's Cup. He made it clear that he hated journalists, and he spent much of his time on air expressing his contempt for the way the stories he presented had been constructed. In press interviews, he delighted in ramming the point home:

> [Clive] doesn't watch much television, has given up newspapers and thinks journos are pretty thick
> 'Journalists in Sydney are all smart arsed.
> They make things up but when you have a go at them they go: 'Ahhh, mate! Oh maaaate! You just ran over my wife? Aaaah mayte, C'mon maayte. Let's have a drink. Everyone's wife gets run over sooner or later. She wasn't gunna live forever, maayte, carm onnn ...' (Anderson 1992: 6)

About his own role as newsreader, he could be pretty scathing too:

> It's silly sitting there, reading something to someone. Can't they buy a
> newspaper for themselves? Why should 1 have to do it for them?
> Should I pop around and wash them in their baths, dress them in the
> mornings? (Lyons 1988: 3)

His contempt for the institution that paid him allowed him to comment
freely on the news, and particularly on the manner of its reporting. He
would foreground such standard continuity devices as the use of establishing shots, noddies, and voiceovers, and ridicule their deployment in the
stories he was introducing. Not surprisingly, journalists hated him as much
as he hated them and objected to his treatment of their work (Glover,
1988: 12).

Robertson's ridicule of particular news content was not entirely programmatic, despite the fact that many regarded it as a form of political bias.
His criticisms of the media, however, were principled and suggested he
was contemptuous of the way it promoted personalities, even though he
was himself a direct beneficiary of this (Wilson, 1994: 35). It would be
hard to deny that Clive Robertson, when compared with the coolly formal
persona of traditional newsreaders, gave a highly self-promoting performance. Nonetheless, it would also be possible to argue that Robertson
defended traditional journalism by attacking the trivialisation of television
news, the spurious routinisation of its production of realism, and the lack
of depth in its reporting. While offering a deliberately entertaining performance of eccentricity, he also invited his audience to endorse his critique of the regime within which his own program operated. He defended
the values of quality, 'truthful' news against the imperatives of entertainment; his own performance happily undermined the constructedness of
the authority of the presenter (he was particularly prone to long, rumina-
tive pauses while he considered what to do next); and he exposed the discursive processes which constructed the news. Paradoxically, far from
alienating his audience in this way (and it was, remember, still a news audience), Robertson built a strong and loyal following which stayed with him,
despite his several mysterious 'disappearances' of a week or so at a time.

Given all of this, and although his was certainly a subversive performance in terms of its pushing the entertainment rather than the news potential of the timeslot, one could easily regard Robertson's view of the

function of the news as nevertheless quite old fashioned and elitist – in the terms that Catharine Lumby might use to describe him (I am thinking of the comments I quoted from her work in the previous chapter). Interestingly, it was not universally understood this way at the time. For some within the television industry, it was the eccentricity and subversive comedic style that was the key to Robertson's success. The similarity of Robertson's persona to that of Peter Finch's newsreader in the 1976 film *Network* might have suggested that his audience appeal depended upon a liberal weariness with the hype and triviality of the news medium itself – that is, along the lines of Franklin's 'newszak' critique. Robertson's daring to rail at its practices while actually working in the belly of the beast must have looked heroic to this audience. Over at Channel 9, however, it was Robertson's disrespect – his mischievous disruption of the seriousness of the news and its consequent redefinition as a genre of talk/entertainment – that was deemed most responsible for the 'cult' success of *Newsworld*.

What Channel 9 sought was a way to produce a similarly transgressive intervention but one which could break out of the 'cult' demographic. Their choice as presenter was Graham Kennedy. It was not such an off-the-wall choice. Kennedy had experienced more success with late night television than anybody, and he had also sat in as host of Seven's news and talk program *11AM* in 1985 for a couple of months. Press reports suggested:

> [I]t would not be a surprise if it [*Graham Kennedy's News Show*] turned out to be almost identical to *Newsworld* – because Graham Kennedy has already had a trial run at such a program ... His often irreverent comments on the news and a general refusal to maintain a pose of high decorum was a precursor of what Clive Robertson does now. (Murphy 1988: 24)

Graham Kennedy's News Show commenced in late April 1988, Kennedy sharing the desk with journalist Ken Sutcliffe. The initial framework was ragged, Kennedy dropping his seasoned gags and then moving on to read news items. This represented a direct affront to the authority of news, the established nostrums of the importance of the impartiality and sobriety of the newsreader, and the sense that there were aspects of news that must be quarantined off from the discourses of entertainment. The critical reactions were immediately very strong:

Graham Kennedy's style was as irreverent [as Clive Robertson's], but in worse taste, especially when the opening comedy repartee ran seamlessly, too seamlessly, into a report on the death sentence passed on the Nazi war criminal Ivan the Terrible (John Demanjuk). 'They threw that one at us', he said, by way of explanation for the twitches that threatened to break into a grin [...] We were promised freshened news, but we were given a repeat of the 6 pm bulletin. We were promised wit but were given cheap and contrived verbal slapstick. (Hooks 1988: 14)

Similarly, in *The Australian*, Patrick Whitely wrote:

[I]t is good to see the light side of the news and not to take things too seriously all the time, but you do not laugh when a man almost falls to his death from a cliff like Kennedy's sidekick Ken Sutcliffe did on the opening show. (1988: 13)

It was impossible to disguise the fact that the news was being played for laughs, and that this was both irresponsible and unlikely to rate. Kennedy mugged at the camera in his familiar bug-eyed way, but Sutcliffe – the straight man supposed to uphold the values of hardcore news – simply fed him lines and sniggered sycophantically at Gra-Gra's gags. The conceptual shift required to watch Kennedy reading the news proved simply beyond the viewers' capacity and very quickly this strategy was changed. A 'real' news reader, George Donikian, was wheeled in to read the bulletins while Kennedy and Sutcliffe dealt with the lighter items and chatted amiably to the crew. The status of the news was protected by this strategy, even though successive newsreaders had to endure the chiacking of Kennedy and Sutcliffe (later, John Mangos) before getting on with their serious job.

This formal separation of news and comedy stopped *Graham Kennedy's News Show* from being embarrassing, and allowed it to build its own format. Another element was needed before it could hum along smoothly: an audience. It had become obvious that Kennedy's playing to Sutcliffe or Mangos, or to the crew, not only excluded the home viewer but also implicitly denied the centrality of comedy to the genre the show was developing. The addition of a studio audience acknowledged the centrality of comedy, firmly established that certain news items would be used as comedy material rather than as information, and allowed a relatively firm distinction to be drawn between the 'news' and the 'show' elements of *Graham Kennedy's News Show*. Significantly, this title was dropped during the first season and replaced by a title which signified a more 'tonight' or talk-show format, *Graham Kennedy Coast to Coast*.

Once the format was set and this hybridised genre became legible to its audience, the program began to rate. By August of the first year it had knocked off Channel 10's *Don Lane's Late Night Australia* and was closing in on Robbo. By the end of 1988 it was winning some nights, and by the end of 1989 it effectively had the timeslot to itself. However, Kennedy did not return for a new season in 1990; the show ran with Gretel Killeen as host for a few weeks but folded on 6 April 1990. In a testament to the wonderful flexibility of television programming, *Robbo's World Tonight* commenced on Channel 9 on 9 April the same year.

Kennedy's show was a radical challenge to news conventions and to the way in which the competition between the conflicting imperatives of information and entertainment had hitherto been negotiated. Often, it was very entertaining television but its effect on the credibility of the news can only have been corrosive. Kennedy did not stand for the traditional news values that Robbo implicitly supported; Kennedy endorsed the imperatives of entertainment and was contemptuous of the liberal-ethical pretensions of 'quality' journalism. Kennedy's humour was broad, slapstick, and conventional; Robertson's was black, private and subversive. While both operated as media personalities, only Kennedy seemed entirely comfortable with that. Both competed in developing hybrid genres which put news to work in novel and slightly transgressive ways. While their respective approaches may have carried contradictory implications for the future of news, the result of their contest for viewers was to significantly increase the total audience in that timeslot – a rare feat in television.

Once late night became an area for audience development, further strategies were tried. The success of Robertson and Kennedy sparked the introduction of another competitor who combined Robertson's slightly subversive comic touch with Kennedy's populism. Steve Vizard's *Tonight Live* (Seven Network) opted for the conventional format of 'Tonight' shows but included an invitation to those who were considering moving across from Kennedy and, later, Robbo – news updates from Jennifer Keyte. Vizard's target audience, however, was precisely the demographic that did not turn on the news – young adults, Generation X, the core audience of the hit satirical comedy show of the moment, *Fast Forward*, which is where Vizard had developed his following. The hook to catch *them* came from the US. Vizard's *Tonight Live* borrowed liberally from the successful late night American talk shows hosted by David Letterman and Arsenio Hall. From Letterman came the verbal tags and identifying mannerisms of the host, and some of the format items such as the viewer faxes; from Hall came the resident band, the integration of vertiginous wide shots of the whole set and the audience into the program, and the use of a wildly revved up studio audience to give the sense of excitement, liveness and 'cult' exclusivity. The local flavour came from the degree to which the audience were integrated into the performance of the show: people were regularly pulled out of the audience for apparently spontaneous segments, audience members engaged in conversation with the host and selected members of the audi- ence at home were visited by a roving camera, 'Viewercam'. As is the case with most shows in the history of the 'Tonight show' format, the audience were invited to be on the telly, and the following the show developed does seem to have something to do with this slightly unpredictable and extremely populist potential – of becoming part of the spectacle of tele- vision. Much as had been the case with the target demographic's favourite program of the 80s, *Hey Hey It's Saturday* (Nine Network), however, the key contradiction for *Tonight Live* to negotiate was how to structure its 'unpredictable' format so that it could be produced routinely (see Turner, 1989: 25–27),

Tonight Live was dramatically successful, and the format itself con- tinues today – more or less intact – in *Rove*. Launched in January 1990, the show achieved an audience share of 42.3 per cent (47 per cent in Melbourne, Vizard's home town) in its first year. In 1992 Vizard picked up the Gold Logie, and even in the last year of production (1993), when Vizard used a succession of guest hosts to relieve his boredom, it was still attracting 30.2 per cent of the sets in use during its timeslot. In some respects pure late night chat, *Tonight Live* was initially positioned as a direct response to Robertson and Kennedy (at the time the show was pre- miered, Kennedy was still supposed to be returning for a new season of *Coast to Coast*), and so the network encouraged the view that it would have a strong news and current affairs content. However, as was the case with Kennedy's show (but less so with Robertson), the interviews remained firmly in the chat rather than the current affairs genre and the news spot existed in an awkward tension with the rest of the format.

The news spot was a regular component of the show, but it never sat easily within it. Originally, newsreader Jennifer Keyte walked on set for her segment, the camera angles collaborating with the personality profiles that talked of her as a 'leggy', 'rangy' ex-model. The raucous Vizard audience treated her the same way, and the news spot started to fall apart, as a media report at the time suggests:

> Seven ... is worried that Keyte, who earns around $130 000, will have her attempt to be seen as credible hurt by her appearances as the leggy 'newsreader with the mostest' on the Steve Vizard show. Keyte was forced recently to hose down a studio audience in uproar over a news item about the death of 15,000 chickens. 'It's not really a funny story', she told them. Since she took over as main [6 o'clock bulletin] news-reader, Vizard producers have stopped audience whoops and wolf whis-tles as she sits at her desk. (Wilmoth and Button 1990: 6)

Eventually, Keyte's entrance was cut, and Vizard threw to her already seated at her desk. Keyte's performances always maintained her detach-ment from the rest of the show, her manner consistently refusing com-plicity with Vizard – even in their set-ups together at the end of some shows: '[I]f I were to get more involved in the mayhem of the show and let my guard down, it would be very hard to function again as a believable newsreader', she said in an interview for *Mode Australia* (Reines, 1990: 20). Nevertheless, she also accepted that the distinction between news and entertainment was blurring: 'I think there's a very fine line between the two mediums' (20).

The category of news as then performed on Australian television was subverted by these three programs, each in its own way, and to varying effect: Robertson enacted a liberal critique of the constructedness of tele-vision news conventions, Kennedy exploited the news shamelessly as a straight feed for his one-liners, and Vizard incorporated it as one compo-nent of the required entertainment mix for his youth-oriented audience. While all three, in effect, collaborated in expanding the news content avail-able on television, this collaboration was not in the service of a consistent critique of the quality of conventional news-casting nor even a consistent call for a more entertaining news service. It was more contradictory than that, and it produced some unforeseen and longstanding consequences. While the major consequence of this history was the installation of 10.30 pm news services on all the commercial channels, it was ultimately to be a news service of the most conventional kind. Even though the Seven Network persisted with its attempt to attract the youth audience to the timeslot with *The Times* and *Denton*, it ultimately accepted defeat and installed a conventional late night bulletin in December, 1994.

Ironically, then, while it was the competition between news and entertainment that built the audience for these timeslots, and while the key attribute of the history I have described is an iconoclastic hybridisation of genres, the late night news formats that survived were not, comparatively, particularly entertaining. Nonetheless, this was a series of lively attempts to do something fresh and original that did attract new audiences to news and current affairs. It made the presentation of the news both newsworthy and interesting, it created an audience that did not exist previously, and it changed the commercial shape of the television schedule. Something similar is needed right now.

Desperately seeking ...

The second aspect I want to consider here is the younger audience's apparent lack of interest in television news and current affairs, something we have already briefly discussed in chapter 1. Again, this is routinely assumed to be the consequence of a resistance to boring, conventional news programming. The clear preference among young people for finding their current affairs content in entertainment programming tends to support such an assumption. However, it may not be quite that simple. In this section, I want to return to the mid-1990s again, because this is probably the only time when free-to-air television actively set out to win over the young adult audience to its current affairs programming. As is even more radically the case now, the young audience for news and current affairs was in decline during the 1990s, and the issue had been attracting attention for almost a decade. During the first half of the 1990s, it was widely noted that young people – the so-called Generation X – were watching the network news less and less. In the US, surveys claimed that while 35 per cent of people aged 21–24 watched *The Simpsons* and 29 per cent watched *CNN*, only 20 per cent watched the ABC's network news bulletin. Further, between 1980 and 1993, the percentage of viewers between 18 and 34 watching commercial network news in the US had dropped more than 45 per cent (Katz 1994, 31–33). In Australia, a 1993 Clemenger survey found no news bulletins among the top 20 television programs for the 16–24-year-old age group; in 1983, there had been three (Sternberg 1995: 46–7). As we have seen already, these trends have continued into the 21st century. The difference, however, is that in the mid-1990s the networks still thought there was something they could do about it.

Media researcher Jason Sternberg's work at this time focused upon this trend, and attempted to interpret it to the media industries.[3] He highlighted the urgency of the problem with television news: he pointed out that while the decline in newspaper readership among Generation X was not as great as for the Australian population as a whole (28 per cent as against 31 per cent), in television news the reverse was true. Sternberg cited with approval Jon Katz's explanation of the same pattern in America:

> ... it's hard to think of anything the [news] industry could have done to ignore or alienate younger consumers that it hasn't done, isn't still doing and doesn't plan to do in the future. It has resisted innovative design, clung to a deadly monolithic voice, refused to broaden or alter its definitions of news and trashed the world of the young at every opportunity. (1995: 47)

Sternberg saw it as a format issue as well as a content one, and went on to argue that new generic structures, new visual styles, and embracing some of the textual attributes of postmodernity had the capacity to change this situation. He nominated several television current affairs shows of the time, such as *Attitude*, *The Times*, and the short-lived *Level 23* as programs which had the capacity to create a new, alternative, style of youth-oriented current affairs by hybridising and fracturing traditional genres:

> A current affairs program like *The Times*, for instance, deals with 'serious' issues in the political economy, yet manages to shatter official news genre expectations. *The Times* does not necessarily draw on tabloidism's genre conventions: just its irreverence and transgressive play. In this sense, *The Times*' form can be seen to draw just as heavily

on the disjunctive play of music-videos and postmodern magazines like
The Face and *i-D*, as it does on news genres and clearly demonstrates
those ideas of free-floating meanings, metamedia, pastiche, transgres-
sion, sensation and spectacle ... (1995: 46)

These are resonant stylistic markers, particularly the reference to the visual
styles of *The Face* and *i-D*. Sternberg applauded the fact that these programs' attempts to make news look different – exploiting the whole of the
screen with graphic styles lifted from music magazines and computer programs, speeding up cutting rhythms, raising the level of background noise,
and allowing different sources of information to compete and overload in
the way of computer screen graphics – was designed to appeal to a youth
audience. The ratings evidence would suggest that the attempts were only
moderately successful, but they did establish a new repertoire of signifiers
of 'the contemporary' for a wide range of television programming. Hence,
their gradual appropriation later on by pay TV news channels, lifestyle programming, and even, on occasions, more sober programs such as *The 7.30
Report*.

Sternberg's contemporary account is useful, and it is worth following it
up with closer analysis of these programs. When the ABC's *Attitude* commenced in 1993, it promoted itself as original, 'in your face', current affairs
aimed at the youth market. Much was made of the fact that none of its
reporters were over 25, and that they intended to give youth 'a voice'.
Interestingly, most profiles at the time noted how personally conventional
these young presenters were, how 'morally and politically correct' they
seemed to their older colleagues at the ABC (Gill, 1993, 2). Their product
was innovative, however. *Attitude* based its stories around social attitude
research commissioned from AGB McNair on particular issues: youth
suicide, drug-taking, the Australian music industry and so on. While the
reporter compiled the story and appeared in a small, brief still at its head,
they did not appear on camera subsequently and most of their questions
were edited out. What I have been calling the authority of the presenter
was displaced, and thereby one of the key tools of commercial current
affairs discarded. Instead of speaking to the host, presenter or reporter who
then acted as interpreters for the audience, the interviewees enjoyed direct
access to the audience, telling their stories straight to camera in relaxed
bites. This realist documentary style was mixed against highly active, even

intrusive, visuals. Graphics ran information in front of or behind interviewees, experts were confined to a corner of the screen while visual noise
packed the remainder, camera angles were often bizarre and unconventional, and the speed of editing and the flow of information demanded
close attention from the viewer. *Attitude*'s visual style was more arty than
'in your face', though, and while they often took courageous and unfashion-
able positions – as in stories on youth unemployment and second-wave
feminism – they did so without being especially abrasive or opinionated. In
fact, while *Attitude* was a critical success from the moment it commenced,
it always seemed to be a little anodyne: the format's reliance on what was
really a standard attitude survey meant that it often found itself locked out
of the possibility of offering a judgement, of suggesting an interpretation of
what it had discovered. Not a weakness shared by most of the other current
affairs programs screening at the time – these included *Hinch* and *Alan
Jones Live!* – this problem became more damaging when *Attitude* moved
to its Saturday night timeslot for the third series in 1994.

The 9.30 pm Wednesday timeslot had previously been occupied by the
current affairs discussion program *Couchman* and this had allowed
Attitude to deal with adult issues explicitly and without compromise.
While it was continually being threatened with the axe over its first two
series in this timeslot, and while this was the special event timeslot for the
ABC and so programs occupying it had to accept being bumped for the odd
week here and there, *Attitude* attracted reasonable ratings (around 14 in
1993). It was making news and attracting strong reviews in the press.
Nevertheless, when it commenced its third season in 1994 it was reduced
to half an hour (from 40 minutes in the original series), and was scheduled
at 8.00 pm Saturday in direct competition with *Hey Hey It's Saturday* – at
that time, something of an institution for younger viewers. Suicidal programming perhaps, but *Attitude* was immediately preceded by re-runs of
Frontline – itself a favourite with that demographic – which might have
been expected to deliver a reasonable-sized audience. The producers were
bravely upbeat about the new 'lighter touch' this earlier timeslot would
require: 'We will cover issues, but we'll do them in a way which is not off-
putting. A lot of current affairs issues beat you around the head and lecture
you and try to harass you and try to force opinions on you' (Couch, 1994).
From 'in your face' to 'feel good' current affairs, it was a long way from the
original conception of the program. Despite a first episode on two young

stand-up comedians which maximised the tie-in with *Frontline*, *Attitude* sacrificed much of its distinctiveness for this timeslot.

Although you would have to say that ultimately it was not a success in reaching the youth demographic it sought, *Attitude* was an impressively different take on current affairs television. Importantly, it showed what current affairs might be like if it was stripped of some of the prevailing conventions: the dependence on the authority of the presenter, the structural centrality of the producer's angle rather than the authority of the subject telling the story, and a visual presentation composed solely through the discourses of news and documentary rather than through the more entertainment-oriented strategies of narrative and drama. It also changed the look of current affairs, depending on a higher degree of visual literacy and radically speeding up the transactions that occurred between the viewer and the visuals on the screen. At its worst worthy, and at its best exhilaratingly fresh, *Attitude* did well enough in the market and in the industry to encourage a commercial channel to try a similar initiative.

Channel 7 launched *The Times* in 1994, implicitly acknowledging its lineage by promoting itself as 'TV with attitude'. Like its precursor, *The Times* had a chequered career with minor changes in host and format but major shifts in timeslot over the three years it struggled along. When it began, interviews with the production team positioned the program as 'filling the void in unconventional late night current affairs shows left by Clive Robertson and Graham Kennedy's *Coast to Coast*'. Like Robertson, *The Times* was going to have its opinions: 'this program is quite open about the fact that it has an opinion and, like it or lump it, that's what we'll do' (Plunkett, 1994: 1). They also set out to produce a very different house style, a 'cartoon or magazine-like production' which broke away from thinking of the visual style of current affairs programs solely through the established television news conventions:

> Seven said our brief was to create something different. There's a large audience out there able to take in more information than just a talking head in a studio. There might be three or more sources of information being presented simultaneously on *The Times*: headlines, captions, superimposed images, plus the main camera image. The headlines could take on a satirical edge, or they might play it straight; it's all a question of balance and keeping up the pace. (Plunkett 1994: 2)

Significant here was the audience's assumed comfort with other screen technologies: the need for multiple information sources and maintaining the speed of visual stimuli and information delivery both seem to assume computer as well as televisual literacies.

While it, too, failed to build a strong audience following, in many other respects *The Times* was successful. It certainly looked like no other current affairs program. Its disregard for 'objectivity' produced clearly opinionated but also vigorously engaging stories and it made a considerable use of wit and satire within, or in counterpoint to, its narratives. *The Times* sought a youthful audience through an upbeat, irreverent and playful style; there is anecdotal evidence this was successful as a mode of address but it was never sufficiently evident from the ratings. The frequent changes in time slot cannot have helped it build its audience – although being bracketed by *Denton* in its time slot for most of 1995 must have helped a little. The frontman was a problem, too, I suspect. Although the first series used Neil Mercer –more or less suitably sharp and streetwise – the final series' choice of Paul Barry was less convincing. No matter how long Paul Barry hung around Kings Cross in casual clothes he still looked as if he was working for *Four Corners*.

One would hope that these programs will not be the last attempts to attract a youth audience back to current affairs. For what it's worth, I think it is clear that the earnest and slightly preachy approach of *Attitude* did not work as well for this audience as the brasher, more cynical approach taken by *The Times*, There may be a lesson in that. The programs' value lay, however, in their trialling of alternative models for television current affairs. This is certainly the value I saw in dealing with them at some length in this book. *Attitude* and *The Times* invented formats which were entertaining, fast moving, visually interesting, and informative. This was achieved without foot-in-the-door tactics, hidden cameras, chequebook journalism or high-profile presenters. *Attitude* gave its audiences (apparently) direct access to its subjects. Their model was the 'objective' attitude survey identified with the empirical and 'value-free' social sciences; their achievement was to make this interesting and coherent in a 40-minute current affairs show. *The Times*' approach was directly contrary; its research produced an opinion which the program took openly and clearly, structuring the treatment it gave to an issue. For many of its audience (according to my students at the time), this usefully discarded some of the more spurious aspects of the tradition of objectivity that was responsible for so much of what they regard as the hypocrisy of the present formations of current affairs.

It is this connection that seems most important to this history. Rather than simply setting out to make current affairs more entertaining to their target audience – by tweaking the stylistic conventions and modernising the visual design – both these programs set out to establish their difference from the conventional current affairs programming currently on offer. The opposition between news and entertainment was not the key guiding principle here; rather, it was an opposition between what had become the conventional forms of news and current affairs production and the search for an alternative that was less constructed, less self-interested, and more socially and politically engaged.

What we can learn from Michael Moore

Among the lessons from these histories is that, at the simplest, news and entertainment may not be the only core categories we need to work with here. For a start, these histories suggest that news and entertainment do not have to be mutually exclusive or even antagonistic categories. Further, they demonstrate that the traditional modes of news and current affairs do not of themselves guarantee journalistic 'quality', nor are they the only representational strategies which will address and satisfy a serious news and current affairs audience. Finally, they remind us that there are more ways of presenting news and current affairs in a credible and entertaining manner than are currently available to us on Australian television. Let me expand on this a little further.

As I was writing this chapter, Michael Moore's film *Fahrenheit 9/11* was topping the US box office on its opening weekend; in Australia it became the highest grossing documentary ever screened. My teenage son and daughter asked to be taken to see it; they had never asked to see a documentary in the cinema before (although they did hire *Bowling for Columbine* from the video store some time earlier). My eldest daughter, now in her twenties, has never taken much interest in politics, but she went to see it too. Now all three are going back to the video store to hire copies of Michael Moore's current affairs television series, *The Awful*

Truth. They are members of the demographic least interested in politics within a population that, we are told, has lost interest in politics too. They are definitely interested in the way Michael Moore presents politics, however.

The techniques used in *Fahrenheit 9/11* are similar to those Moore used in *Bowling for Columbine,* and in his television series *The Awful Truth* and *TV Nation.* Typically, Moore takes up a particular political position as his opening premise, expecting his audience to share that position. There is nothing objective about his practice at all; indeed, he marshals his evidence in highly motivated ways – through focused interviews, through public archive journalistic research, and through a persuasive narrative built by the editing as much as by the argument. There is no doubt that Michael Moore employs many of the techniques we identified as tabloid earlier in this book (hence his critics' complaints that he presents extremely selective accounts of the truth and scores with 'cheap shots'). He regularly uses ambush interviews or walk-ins to confront his targets in their place of business, and he is especially fond of setting up media stunts aimed at embarrassing and ridiculing his targets. Sometimes, as was the case with his approach to the supermarket chain selling bullets to minors in *Bowling for Columbine,* this produces a result: they agree to take the bullets off the shelf. *The Awful Truth* used such stunts, and occasionally such outcomes, as its stock in trade. Interestingly, they are performed without quite the level of self-important drama we might connect with a Mike Munro (*A Current Affair*) walk-in. Where Munro performed the walk-in as a means of demonstrating the power of his program,[4] Moore's unkempt, shambling, and disarmingly respectful approach disavows (perhaps disingenuously) his mediated power and his personal authority as a media figure. The stunts themselves are cannily contrived for their spectacular effect: the look on the face of the Congressman, in *Fahrenheit 9/11,* who is asked to sign up his son for service in Iraq, spoke volumes. The point of these stunts is to produce such a media moment – in this case, to demonstrate the reality of the Congressman's taken-for-granted privilege in a memorable manner on film. At such moments, Moore works more like a media activist, or even a 'culture jammer', than a journalist; it is not at all disinterested, but neither is it merely self-serving.

A key difference between Moore's deployment of tabloid tactics and spectacular stunts and their deployment by most Australian current affairs programs is that he uses them primarily against the strong and the powerful; almost uniformly his targets are big companies or institutions and elite individuals. Dressed in a way that announces his ordinariness, adopting a persona that may be dogged but which is not particularly assertive or threatening, he uses the camera in a highly motivated, rather than a documentary, manner as a means of delivering power to his audience. It looks like documentary, though. The hand-held camera irresistibly signifies immediacy and authenticity to the viewer, while also discomfiting its subjects with the implicit threat of media exposure. The method delivers to us a political version of *Candid Camera*, where the viewer-voyeur is placed momentarily in control over those who ordinarily exercise political power. Significantly, when he deals with those who are subordinated in the political system, Michael Moore tends towards the tolerant and sympathetic – even when they are representatives of positions he opposes. His core concerns are a long way from the world of the bad neighbour and the cheating video-repairman and so he is really only interested in these people as the effects of power. Finally, Moore does not even bother to pretend to be running an open-ended investigation. He constructs himself as a crusader; his function is to attempt to intervene in, and if possible, correct a situation he has already decided is wrong.

Clearly, this is a powerful mix. The audience appearing in *The Awful Truth* responds to Michael Moore as to a cult hero. This audience, importantly, is relatively youthful, attracted by his anti-establishment positioning and by the discursive components which indicate that he is addressing *them* first and foremost: the use of contemporary rock music, particularly the political sub-genre of American punk, and a contemporary verbal idiom that connects him with youth and with the street. His book attacking Bush's America is called *Dude, Where's My Country?*, after the popular teen film, *Dude, Where's My Car?* If the intellectuals don't like such a populist strategy for such a serious topic, then so be it, he seems to say: his primary audience is those who do – precisely those who are alienated by more conventional approaches to current affairs journalism. The mystery, perhaps, is why this doesn't come across as cynical or patronising or just plain unconvincing – given Moore's age and his lack of any kind of youth culture 'cool' at all. My hunch is that what makes his work convincing is his spectacular cheek: what creates *this*, in turn, is the daunting, sometimes even iconic, status of so many of his targets. Categorically, Moore takes on the targets that network news and current affairs is most disinclined to attack – major political and commercial institutions, and powerful individuals. Classic populist tactics, perhaps, but their effectiveness for their audience holds some lessons, I think, about what is being asked of current affairs by this audience today, and what is wrong with what is being delivered. Simply, programs today don't care to take on the things that audiences believe really matter, and they don't care to challenge the powerful. Importantly, Moore does not come across as someone who is intent merely on producing a body of programming or building a competitive brand. The difference between Moore's constructed persona and that of his commercial television presenter counterparts (and I admit this could be a pretty fine distinction) is his evident engagement with the issues he explores. His audience's tolerance for the manipulative methods he uses may well be related to this: that is, maybe they appreciate the fact that Moore appears to want his audience to care about the issue at hand and that he is prepared to exploit any of the available conventions and approaches in order to achieve this result.

Perhaps, in the end, Michael Moore appeals because, by and large, he is not what contemporary journalism has become. Passionate, committed, prepared to bend the rules in pursuit of political change rather than merely a high-rating program – I think these might fit as descriptors for much of what *TDT* did in the early days of current affairs television in Australia – but they are not descriptors for the kinds of news and current affairs we are used to consuming today.

Earlier in this chapter, in the discussion of current affairs' attempt to reach the youth audience, I made the point that these programs seemed to have deliberately differentiated their approach from that of conventional contemporary journalism – attempting to generate new ways of dealing with news and current affairs that were not the ways of journalism. The neologism 'post-journalism' was coined to refer to the news media's shift away from the practices and ethics of traditional journalism: the usual culprits for this shift include chequebook journalism, the influence of public relations and promotions, and the submerging of the imperatives of news beneath the demand for entertainment. Also implicated is an underlying scepticism about the extent to which the social-democratic 'mission' of journalism can survive such changes – pointing to the declining respect in which the profession of journalism is held. I used the term 'post-journalism' myself in 1996 to refer to the distance that was emerging between the content of traditional journalism and the emerging trends in current affairs at that time. Drawing on John Hartley's suggestion in *The Politics of Pictures* (1992) that journalism now occurred within a 'post-truth' society, the view I took then was that commercial television current affairs now operated within a 'post-journalism' production culture (Turner, 1996c: 88): where the values of journalism had given way to other commercial considerations. I would argue now that the issue is not just a matter of news selling out to entertainment. It is also that journalism seems no longer interested in issues of political and social substance, nor is it performed with the kind of open passion and commitment that has attracted audiences to Michael Moore.

I believe this has been particularly relevant for the younger market demographics. Since journalism itself lacks credibility with the younger audience it has become necessary for new formats aimed at this audience to clearly separate themselves from that tradition. As a result then, and as we have seen, younger audiences watch *Enough Rope* and *The Panel* rather than *The 7.30 Report* or *Sixty Minutes*. In my view, this happens because news matters, not because it doesn't. These new formats are largely entertainment formats, it is true, but they are also marked by a highly sceptical, alienated, attitude to established politics and its representation that is actually the reverse of disinterest. Indeed, these formats tend to pitch to a particular political demographic, too, taking for granted a (usually left-liberal) shared political orientation. There are dangers, of course, in that those who lap up Michael Moore or the political preferences of *The Panel* would probably deplore the existence of their right wing or conservative counterparts. Nevertheless, in the trade between news and entertainment across the formats available at present, it is not at all obvious that these entertainment-driven formats are any less politically or socially engaged than some of their more conventional current affairs competitors. Rather, it is possible that their audiences actually take news far more seriously than those who watch *Today Tonight*, and that is why they don't watch it themselves. Perhaps we have moved on to a world where news and current affairs can still pull big audiences, but they can't do it any longer in the name of journalism.

So, is this the end of journalism as we know it? While we look at this particular sector of the media – the youth-oriented talk shows on television – it is easy to support the kinds of conclusions I have been working on here. When we look at some other locations, however, things can appear to be playing out quite differently. For instance, in the print media, it is the 'quality' end of town that is thriving, with the Fairfax stable and *The Australian* outlasting their tabloid competitors. Even in television, the figures for *The 7.30 Report* and *Australian Story* are currently running slightly against the grain of the decline we have been discussing in relation to current affairs programming on the commercial networks – and it is to the situation of the ABC's current affairs programming I want to turn in the following chapter. However, as I close this chapter, it might be worth pointing to an even more dramatic shift that may be on its way to us. In the US, according to the 5 August (2004) edition of ABC Radio National's *The Media Report*, the trend in radio is all the other way. This is how presenter Mick O'Regan put it:

> So, if the number of people watching commercial TV current affairs is declining, is the conclusion that people aren't interested in serious news analysis? One argument suggests what they want is more reality programs. More people renovating backyards, and trying to become pop stars. Less serious discussion of complex political and social ideas. But is it a question of what people want or what they're offered? In the United States, where much of the media focus is on the rise and rise of the Fox News Channel, another distinct trend is becoming clear; people want quality information, especially in the current international political context.
>
> One of the key beneficiaries is National Public Radio, which has seen its audience grow by 64% in the last five years, from 13 million to 22 million. The network's flagship programs, *Morning Edition* and *All Things Considered*, are now the second and third most listened to national radio programs in the United States.[5]

Of course, I should point out that the most listened to national radio program in the US is still Rush Limbaugh, but nevertheless this is a staggering development. This is a network which has a commitment to traditional notions of quality, which insists on what they call 'fact-based' reporting (as distinct from opinion, even the opinion of interviewees[6]), and which does not respond to what its CEO calls 'mass taste or to mass culture or to pop culture'. This is the antithesis of the developments I have been describing in this chapter, and it has built its audience dramatically. There is a suggestion that this trend has been exacerbated by the interest in 'serious presentation of fact-based reporting' that has followed 9/11, but nonetheless, this is a spectacular shift in audience preferences. It underlines the difficulty of making blanket pronouncements about such shifts with any confidence in their comprehensiveness. 'News entertainments' are certainly in the ascendancy, but there is no shortage of other directions available or other models in play. In this case it should also underline the difficulty of claiming too much for the postjournalism idea: that journalism is passé and we have moved on. Clearly, while there may be many ways of doing what journalism has done, the old ways are still around and still attract an audience. The problem I have been addressing in this chapter is about what strategies may be available to us if we want to bring more of this audience back to television.

NOTES
1   Network Ten's programming addresses the late teens/young adult demographic as its primary market.
2   The next two sections of this chapter draw substantially on my article, 'Post-journalism: News and Current Affairs Programming from the Late '80s to the mid-90s' (1996: 78–92).
3   When asked by a journalist why young people didn't watch TV current affairs, Sternberg replied: 'I have two words for you: the Paxtons'.
4   By this I mean that the television moment it produces is the primary end in sight – not the assistance of criminal prosecutions, for instance. These performances are meant to demonstrate that the media has a pre-eminent power to shape and intervene in social processes, and thus to reinforce the power and authority of the program and its presenters.
5   <http://www.abc.net.au/rb/talks/8.30/mediarpt/stories/s1167766htm>
6   The way NPR's chief executive, Kelvin Klose, puts it in the interview may help clarify this:

> There's less fact-based reporting going on I believe in the US electronic media than probably at any time since the 1940s, since before World War II. There's a lot of opinion, there's a lot of what we call two-ways, go interview somebody on the street where something happened, or go and interview a reporter where something happened, but don't do the fact-based reporting around the event to tell the context of it, just report the event itself.

CHAPTER FIVE

Bullying the ABC: bias, balance and budgets

The national broadcaster

Next, I want to shift my focus onto the ABC. As we shall see, the problems experienced there are quite different to those experienced in the commercial sector but I will argue that they have had a corrosive effect on the ABC's capacity to present quality television current affairs programs to the national audience.

At the beginning of the televised debate between Mark Latham and John Howard during the 2004 federal election campaign,[1] the Nine Network's Laurie Oakes, the moderator of the debate, introduced proceedings by pointing out that the Nine Network was now the truly 'national broadcaster'. A gratuitous and mischievous thing to say, one would have thought, as the introductory remark to what was, no doubt, a 'national broadcast'. Its particular pertinence lay in the fact that the ABC had, for the first time, declined to co-broadcast the debate at the same time as the Nine Network, choosing to play it later in the evening. The Nine Network was performing this national service, free of commercials, on its own. While that may have given Laurie Oakes' remark some justification, nevertheless you would have to ask who among the audience would care about the long-running campaign to which it referred? That is, Nine's persistent, even obsessive, attempt to consolidate its commercial supremacy as the network where most Australians receive their news by also claiming a form of cultural and political supremacy: the status of the truly 'national' broadcaster.

One of things this incident indicates to me is just how long a moral shadow is cast over the commercial networks by the ABC. No matter how much they deride the ABC's public service mentality, its saturation of middle managers and bureaucratic decision-making, its domination by lefties, lesbians and homosexuals, and its boring 'pc' programming, the commercial networks (and Nine in particular) still can't help resenting the ABC's occupation of the higher ground in debates about the quality of the Australian news media. The commercial news media's default position is a defensive one whenever they are confronted with comparisons of the service they provide to the nation and that provided by the ABC – in terms, particularly, of the quality of the journalism and their commitment to the public good. Understandable, perhaps, but really it is futile. For a start, any comparison of the scale and comprehensiveness of the service provided by the ABC against any one of the commercial networks reveals that the Nine Network's claims are just plain wrong.[2] The ABC's radio network is simply massive, far beyond that of any of its competitors, and provides most of the independent current affairs programming available through that medium (we will return to that briefly later on). In television, while aggregation has removed the ABC's monopolies in some regional areas, its provision of local and regional news is still far ahead of that of any commercial network. (And that's not just in terms of scale, it is quality as well. A Newspoll survey conducted in May and June, 2004, found that 76 per cent of the population believes that the ABC does a very good or quite good job covering issues in country and regional areas, compared to 43 per cent for commercial broadcasters.[3]) While the 24-hour news services on pay TV and, in times of crisis, also on free-to-air have reduced the ABC's edge as the provider of the Australian perspective on international news, the ABC's need for both radio and television content continues to require the maintenance of a larger contingent of foreign correspondents than any of its competitors.

I would acknowledge that while there would be significant differences in story selection, the contents of the ABC news bulletins and that of the Nine Network would not vary in substantial ways. In current affairs, though, national public affairs are overwhelmingly at the centre of the ABC's agenda, while they have more or less gone missing from that of the commercials. And, finally, to return to the context of the federal election, while the Nine Network might want to regard its success in securing the task of hosting the election debate as proof of its status as the national broadcaster, its pleasure must be a little qualified by the damning but undeniable implication that the Nine Network has been preferred over the ABC in recent elections, as well as Laurie Oakes/Ray Martin over Kerry O'Brien, because it suits the politicians' interests: they know they will get an easier ride.

As I have suggested, there is almost a moral dimension to the ABC–commercial comparison at times like these: as if securing the position of the national broadcaster would help legitimate the programming and representational strategies undertaken by commercial news and current affairs across the board. Certainly, conversations with some in the commercial sector reveal their opinion that the ABC's mission is an unrealistically high-minded one and that the way to bring their pretensions down a peg is to accuse them of elitism – of failing to serve the popular audience properly.

The trouble with all of this is that no-one would seriously deny the ABC has performed a vital, even fundamental, role in the development of television news and current affairs in Australia. The ABC trained many of those who have been the key contributors. If we consider those who appear on camera, it would be hard to name more than a few leading figures in Australian television current affairs who did not begin their professional careers at the ABC. Of the Australian television presenters and reporters who have made prominent and long-running careers for themselves, the only ones who come to mind who do not have an ABC pedigree are Jana Wendt and Mike Munro. In terms of program development, the ABC developed the first successful format for short form current affairs, and we discussed that in chapter 2. The ABC also developed the first successful format for longer form current affairs, *Four Corners*, which first went to air in 1961 and is still going strong. It wasn't until 1979 that a commercial counterpart was successful, and *Sixty Minutes'* American-derived format was really an extension of the short form magazine structure rather than an hour-long investigation of a significant issue or story. While *Sixty Minutes* has certainly been the outstanding commercial success in the genre in Australia, however, it has also gradually led the trend towards the more spectacular and sensational versions of television current affairs and away from a public affairs agenda.[4]

The puzzling thing is, however, that although the ABC attracts respect for its foundational and continuing importance in the provision of news and current affairs to Australian audiences, it remains the subject of continual, and vehement, criticism. My research files on the ABC are full of articles debating its institutional structure, its selection of key staff, and its policy positions. By far the largest group of articles, though, is that which deals with accusations of bias, or the lack of balance in the presentation of news and current affairs. Despite the fact that surveys of public attitudes repeatedly express great trust in the ABC (more than express their trust in commercial television),[5] the accusations of bias are regularly made by newspaper columnists as well as by representatives of government. You would seek in vain for a corresponding file of reports on the performance of the commercial networks. Government leaves them alone, by and large, unwilling to offend them unnecessarily. Critics of the Keating Labor government mischievously labelled Senator Graham Richardson, in charge of the media portfolio, the Minister for Channel 9; this was a reference to the influence that Kerry Packer was widely regarded as exercising over media and communications policy.[6] As far as the print media is concerned, I can't recall a newspaper columnist ever taking a commercial network to task for the way they have represented political material.[7] Yet, there have been notorious instances of commercial networks being criticised from the bench in criminal cases for the prejudicial nature of their coverage. The so-called tabloid trend is not normally identified with an exceptionally strong commitment to balance and fairness, and that trend certainly exerts greater influence on the commercial networks than on the ABC. *MediaWatch* thrives on picking up examples of shonky reporting from the commercials as well as the ABC – including the deliberate falsification of important details of the report (the most notorious example resulted in Stuart Littlemore referring to Seven's *Today Tonight* as *Barcelona Tonight* from then on[8]). Further, even with commercial television's self-regulated complaints procedures so heavily skewed against the complainant, some complaints still manage to make it through the courts successfully. So, it is not that the commercial networks are to be trusted always to present material in a balanced or non-prejudicial manner and that the ABC is not. However, only in the case of the ABC is this issue raised as a systemic problem of public concern. Bias, balance and the ABC, is my primary interest, then, in this chapter, and I will start to develop it below.

Political pressure from sitting governments is part of the history of the ABC, and it is structurally embedded in how the network's funding is generated: through annual appropriations by Parliament rather than through an independent source of revenue (such as the licence fee abolished by the Whitlam government). Funding, then, is a crucial means through which the government's political influence is exerted. While many in the commercial sector scoff at suggestions that the ABC is under-funded, and point to the way in which its allocation is eaten up by bureaucratic structures and internal rivalries – and while I have no privileged knowledge of any of this, there are certainly plenty within the ABC who would support such a view – it is not hard to see the effect of the current levels of the national investment in news and current affairs on what appears on the screen. Towards the end of this chapter, I want to address that issue as well.

Bullying the ABC

My research into the ABC's news and current affairs programs has been particularly interested in how the institution's performance has been treated in the press. I found that there were two primary themes running over a long period of time. The first theme refers to disputes involving management, staff, and sometimes government over the political embarrassments caused or likely to be caused by ABC news and current affairs reporting. Political censorship has been regularly attempted, sometimes resisted by management and sometimes not; but history tells us that it is a fact of life for those who have worked at the ABC for any length of time. We have already dealt with some aspects of this issue in chapter 2's discussion of *TDT*. The second theme is related in that it constitutes a specific means through which political pressure is applied, even though it disavows any intention of censoring the ABC's output by invoking instead the principles of objectivity which underpin professional journalism. This theme informs a far more insidious strategy: accusations of a systemic bias in the ABC's news and current affairs reporting, which regard this bias as a reflection of the political preferences of the production culture in the institution.

Readers will recall the period in office of former Minister of Communications, Senator Richard Alston, during which he regularly attacked the ABC's treatment of political issues while also maintaining

regular pressure on management over the content of a range of other programming that he regarded as offending community standards. Pilita Clark
reported in 1998 that during his first two years in office, Alston had written
a total of 180 letters to the ABC, 83 per cent of which dealt with public
complaints about 'offensive, lewd or unsatisfactory programming'.
Interestingly, despite Alston's obsession with political bias around the time
of the second Gulf War, during this period less than eight per cent related
to the political bias 'that he and other ministers [said] .afflicts the ABC'
(Clark, 1998: 5) No matter how strenuously the ABC investigates such
complaints, nor how rigorous the internal monitoring process it puts in
place, it has always been subject to some degree of government pressure.
Ken Inglis, the distinguished historian of the ABC, sees it as a straightforward practice of intimidation that is fundamental to the relation between
government and the ABC, employed by Labor as well as conservative governments of the day. Inglis notes that Dr H.V. Evatt once rang the ABC's
chief executive demanding that a news reader be sacked for having an 'anti-
Labor voice', and that both Dr Evatt and Arthur Calwell were 'keen to
make the ABC a direct instrument of government, empowering a minister
to make sure that no uncongenial, biased voices or other sounds were
transmitted' (Inglis, 1998: 15).

TDT and Four Corners, as the initial current affairs flagships, were
often accused of bias. As far back as 1969, the ABC's chairman, Sir Robert
Madgwick, was forced to defend the accuracy and impartiality of their
news and current affairs programming (Madgwick, 1969: 14–17). Some
observers have taken a longstanding interest in developing the ABC-bias
case. Researcher George Shipp set out to prove bias at TDT in the early
70s, and was still at it during the Gulf War two decades later.[9] Anthony
McAdam was particularly active in the mid-1980s, attempting to root out
what Max Harris called the 'nasty malignancy' of the ABC's left-wing bias,
or what McAdam called 'The ABC's Marxists'.whom he regarded as intent
upon radicalising the ABC's news and current affairs agenda.[10] The Gulf
War generated a raft of commentary on bias and balance, culminating in
Prime Minister Bob Hawke's extraordinary personal attack on an academic
expert used in the ABC's analysis, Professor Robert Springborg. This had
been fuelled by an article written by Gerard Henderson, himself a frequent
contributor to debates about balance and the ABC, which questioned
Springborg's credentials as an independent analyst (1996: 12).

There is a reasonable body of evidence to suggest that governments of both persuasions have regularly attempted to exert pressure on the ABC to secure positive treatment of its members and its policies. Nonetheless, my research would also indicate that the issue of ABC bias has been taken up more frequently and more vehemently by organs from the more conservative side of political debate, such as *Quadrant* magazine, the *IPA Review*, and by conservative newspaper columnists such as Frank Devine and Gerard Henderson. This is not surprising. There is a general view, and certainly some evidence to support it, that journalists tend towards a more critical, left-leaning view of the world and therefore that they would naturally support such a point of view in their reporting of public affairs. John Henningham's 1982 study of television journalists' attitudes has been particularly influential in providing evidence that the vast majority (74 per cent) would locate themselves in the middle or 'a little to the left' of the political spectrum. This broke down to 31 per cent of commercial television journalists and 44 per cent of ABC TV journalists (so we can see where that leads). While 44 per cent of the journalists surveyed voted Labor in the 1980 federal election, he reported, 61 per cent of ABC journalists but only 34 per cent of commercial television journalists voted Labor. Henningham himself was careful to disavow any direct connection between these patterns and political bias in the news, pointing to a number of other, more important, influences on the character of news reporting, such as news values, company policy, commercial pressures and so on (1982: 74–75).[11] Henningham concluded by noting that viewer surveys established that 'most people consider television coverage of political news is balanced – with the ABC earning the highest "fairness" ratings'.[12] Such results are consistent with the kinds of figures we see now, so little has changed in terms of the average viewer's perceptions of the ABC's practice – despite twenty years of allegedly biased and unbalanced reporting.

The fact that Henningham's diagnosis of the journalists' political preferences has stuck around, but his defence of the ABC's fairness has not, is due to the political nature of the continued attack on the ABC's news and current affairs. This is not, despite its appeal to issues of principle, an unmotivated or disinterested attack. The pressure the ABC has faced in recent years is remarkable in showing the government's naked determination to directly influence the content of specific kinds of programming, and to use its control of funding as leverage to that end. Inglis suggests that

Alston went beyond the practice of any of his predecessors in his breach of the convention that the minister must only communicate with the ABC through its chairman and the board – that is, an 'arm's length' separation between the government and the broadcaster must be maintained to ensure that undue political influence is neither exerted nor sought. According to Inglis, Alston was the 'first minister to behave as if the ABC is a government department, not a statutory authority. Instead of staying at arm's length, he ha[d] his fist under the ABC's nose'. This happened on numerous occasions: including the ABC's reporting of the 1998 election, of the 1998 waterfront dispute, of the second Gulf War, and the ABC's decision to continue to televise Sydney's Gay and Lesbian Mardi Gras. Inglis notes that even Frank Devine, *The Australian*'s columnist who tends to lead the pack in ferreting out political bias at the ABC, regarded Alston's direct approach as 'deplorable', questioning the motivation behind the government's attack on the ABC's funding (Inglis, 1998:16); that is, he suggested it was intended to ensure the political subservience of the public broadcaster.[13]

Establishing balance and bias

There are formal professional guidelines to help journalists achieve balance in news and current affairs. At its simplest, balance can be a matter of the amount of air time each of the protagonists in a debate is given: professional best practice is to attempt to provide equal time, if not within the same program then certainly over the period of days during which the issue is being contested. As a result, balance is open to some level of proof: it is possible to total the amount of time given to different points of view and check that they are equivalent. Bias is much harder both to avoid and to prove, because it is so much more interpretative: Bill Peach's sardonic smile became a sign of bias to ABC management during his time at *TDT*; Geraldine Doogue once told me that while she was fronting *Nationwide* she had received letters complaining about the bias expressed through her raising an eyebrow; and the choice of a particular metaphor or figure of speech can be seen as inserting a covert point of view – among the accusations made in Richard Alston's complaints about the ABC's coverage of the second Gulf War in 2003. In many cases, the accusation of bias expresses a general but strenuously held impression that does not depend upon empirical data at all and so it is extremely resistant to being disproved. As a result, it is very hard for the embattled broadcaster to refute such accusations and very easy for its political masters to deploy them as a means of making the broadcasters especially alert to any implications likely to excite criticism of their political coverage. There is no doubt in my mind that the Coalition government, like the government which immediately preceded it, has deliberately used the accusation of bias to bully the ABC into taking a more conservative line in the way it covers politics in general, and controversial political issues in particular. Or, as Errol Simper put it in a 1997 piece in *The Australian*, the ABC is 'not so much biased as bullied' (52).

I think I have good reason to take this view at this time. It would not be radical to suggest that when the Coalition government came to power in 1996, it had the ABC firmly in its sights. Many within the Liberal party blamed the ABC for their 1993 election loss; in particular they blamed Kerry O'Brien's performance as the moderator for the Hewson–Keating televised debate. Hewson reputedly believed that O'Brien favoured Keating in his performance on that day, and this probably remains a key reason why the ABC was never to host an election debate again. According to some commentators, the Coalition believed that the win in 1996 was achieved 'despite the ABC' (Simper, 1998), and retribution was swift. Notwithstanding their election promise of maintaining the ABC's budget, the newly elected government cut $66 million from its funding before commissioning an independent review of the broadcaster's operations. The Mansfield Review of the ABC was set up partly as a means of retrospectively justifying the budget cuts, but it was also meant to produce substantial institutional change. One of the areas where change was foreshadowed was in news and current affairs. Alston had mounted a vigorous attack on bias in the ABC's news reporting, most egregiously on its story selection which he claimed (among other things) was unduly skewed towards the environment and indigenous issues. More dangerously though, one of the issues before Mansfield was the extent to which the ABC's provision of news and current affairs duplicated what was available through the commercial networks in both radio and television. Some in the ABC believed that the clear objective of this part of Mansfield's brief was to find that duplication was indeed occurring, and that therefore there was no need for the ABC to provide these services. According to this account, the government's goal was an extremely radical one: to remove the responsibility for the provision of news and current affairs from the ABC's remit.

I was commissioned to undertake an independent research project which would address this possibility by comparing the news and current affairs programming provided by the ABC with that of the commercial sector, across both radio and television. The aim was to provide the Mansfield review with objective data about the role played by ABC news and current affairs. The survey was conducted in Brisbane, monitoring and analysing two weeks of news and current affairs programming on radio and television in August and September, 1996. I don't need to go into the radio research here, other than to say that it revealed something quite alarming: that there was no current affairs programming other than that provided by the ABC on Brisbane radio. I was surprised to find how comprehensively talkback formats had effectively displaced current affairs programs and how many of their on-air personalities were now expected to perform the task of the journalist. In this medium, then, the proposition that the ABC might no longer be needed was clearly not supportable.

In relation to television, however, it was a little more complicated. The project compared the content of the ABC and Channel 9 evening news bulletins, and the current affairs programs *A Current Affair* (Nine Network) and *The 7.30 Report* (Channel 2). I looked at such issues as the comprehensiveness of the services, their achievement of impartiality and balance, and examined such things as the range of story topics, the mix between local, national and international, the duration of the story, the source (was it derived from their own correspondent, the network, or a news agency?), and what I referred to as the story's relation to the 'news agenda of the day' – which operated more or less as an 'infotainment' index.[14] For those unfamiliar with this kind of work, this research process is called content analysis and it is a standard research method within communications, cultural studies, and the social sciences. It generates quantitative rather than qualitative data: that is, it provides empirical evidence of the numbers of stories presented in a bulletin, for instance, rather than interpretation of how a story has framed or represented a particular issue through its choice of words or visuals. The aims of content analysis are relatively modest but its findings are normally quite hard to dispute without repeating the whole process in order to contest the figures.

Among the general findings of the research was that the commercial channels actually provided more total time for the news, with Channel 10 producing the most; in current affairs, Channel 9 was the largest provider, with Channel 2 coming in second. There were some significant differences in the content of television news between the two sectors. The commercial channel bulletins were dominated by crime: Channel 9's bulletin averaged 24.4 per cent crime stories as against 10.5 per cent on the ABC. The ABC was more interested in politics: 21 per cent of the bulletin, as against Channel 9's 12.3 per cent. More international stories on the ABC came from their own foreign correspondents – 33 per cent to 13.8 per cent – supporting the argument that it provided the greatest proportion of independent Australian reporting of world news. Finally, there was no evidence to support Alston's claim that the ABC's news agenda was unduly influenced by environmental and indigenous affairs. My report put it this way:

> In the period surveyed, ABC news averaged 3% of its bulletin on indigenous affairs and 4.2 % on environmental issues; Channel 9 news averaged 0.5% on indigenous issues and 2 % on environmental issues. In current affairs, Channel 2 averaged 0% on indigenous issues and 2.5% on environmental issues; Channel 9 averaged 0.3 % on indigenous issues and 2.1 % on environmental issues. These figures should put to rest any residual accusations of the privileging of these topics within the ABC, and may rather indicate the need for them to be taken more seriously within the commercial sector.[15]

There were more substantial differences between the two sectors' versions of current affairs. In particular, the shift away from the 'news agenda of the day' was evident in A Current Affair's presenting an average of 28.5 per cent material that was unrelated to the news agenda of the day. The 7.30 Report only scored 3.2 per cent against this criterion.

On the issue of balance and impartiality, the figures actually demonstrated that both sectors operated in an extremely professional manner with the percentage of news stories that could be classified as unbalanced scoring in single figures for both the ABC and Channel 9. I regarded a story as unbalanced if it left out social or political viewpoints that might reasonably be expected to be covered. However, a story was considered balanced

if other stories in the same bulletin provided an appropriate range of competing viewpoints, even if the story itself was unbalanced. The research
was sensitive, too, to the way that the current affairs method of 'devil's
advocate' questioning was a means of allowing a range of opinions to be
presented. The ABC scored higher than its competitor in news with an
average of 3.2 per cent unbalanced stories against an average of 6.4 per
cent, and in current affairs with an average of 1.2 per cent against an
average of 15 per cent. To be fair to the Nine Network results in current
affairs, though, there is a tendency there to even out the allocation of time
by presenting points of view in stories on successive days more often than
is the case on Channel 2, so this figure skews higher than it should as a
result of my focus on balance within the one day's program. There are
many other results I won't go into here, but it is worth quoting the report's
conclusion:

> The project has ... [compared] the service provided by the ABC with
> that of its major competitor in radio and television. When such cross-
> sectoral comparisons occur, they reveal differentials in provision and
> resources; it is not surprising that the ABC is not the largest provider
> of television news and current affairs. Notwithstanding this fact, the
> results establish that the ABC provides the most comprehensive
> service for radio news and for current affairs in both media; it provides
> the most independent service for radio and television news and current
> affairs; and it produces the most impartial and balanced performance
> across all programming surveyed. In some cases the differentials are so
> dramatic as to indicate that, without the presence of the ABC, there
> would be no provision of socially responsible, broadly based news and
> current affairs service to the Australian community. In the crucial areas
> of radio and television current affairs, the evidence supports this con-
> clusion overwhelmingly. (147)

While there were some differences that were important for the Mansfield
review process, the results on balance and bias were absolutely clear:
neither of the media organisations under examination could be accused of
anything less than thoroughly professional conduct, but at a pinch the ABC
could be seen as marginally more successful in its management of its performance than Channel 9 over the two weeks of the survey.

When the report was released, I was given a small taste of what it must be like to work for the ABC. To some commentators and editorial writers, the fact that the accusations of bias had been objectively tested and found to be groundless was no reason at all to disbelieve them. Instead, taking such a position constituted clear evidence of my perfidy, or at best suggested that I had been suborned by the ABC. Since they knew the ABC was biased – that was simply not in doubt – anyone who thought they could prove otherwise was not to be trusted. Media outlets where one might have expected the outcomes of a genuine research project to be respected, such as at the quality end of the press, were happy to print columns, and even editorials, pointing out that no matter what I said there was no question but that the ABC was biased. Even the ABC was leery of reporting the findings in its own programming. I recorded one interview with a reporter from *AM*, who did a thorough devil's advocate number on me ('Why should we believe you?' was the opening question), but the story never made it to air. I have done many interviews on many topics in the media over the years, but this is the only time my credibility as a researcher has been gratuitously challenged.

While the Mansfield review was fortunately persuaded not to divest the ABC of its news and current affairs remit, it was not surprising to find that the issue of bias was not laid to rest. As I said earlier, the issue has been around since before television, and seems to be an institutionalised effect of the structural relation between the ABC and the government of the day. This had not been the first attempt to exonerate the ABC of the charge of presenting biased and partisan news reports, and it was certainly not going to be the last. Indeed, ABC bias flared up as an issue again during 1998, when Alston issued what many regarded as a public threat to the (then) manager of the ABC, Brian Johns, which clearly implied the ABC's funding would not survive an aggressive treatment of the government during the next election campaign. Eventually, yet another independent report was commissioned by the ABC in response to yet another Alston salvo, this time occasioned by the network's treatment of the waterfront dispute between Patricks Stevedores and the Maritime Union of Australia, in which the Industrial Relations Minister Peter Reith had played a particularly murky role.

Professor Philip Bell, of the Media and Communications Unit at the University of New South Wales, was the author of this report and he focused upon the specifics of this case, examining radio and television: in the case of television, he looked at the ABC television news and The 7.30 Report.[16] It was a more sophisticated analysis than I had done two years previously, going beyond content analysis to use more interpretive and linguistic methods. Bell was also canny enough to introduce his report with a discussion of the difficulties involved in demonstrating bias, or establishing balance, given the professional conventions and practices involved. The news media, he pointed out, should be 'biased' towards their assumed audiences or the public, in terms of providing them with information about issues that affect them (1998: 2). That may mean challenging the explanations provided by government. Bell also pointed out that the prevailing conventions for television news mean that reports will be biased towards 'the short term effects of actions, not the long-term causes of complex situations' (4). Finally, he acknowledged the fact that the nature of the medium itself as well as the availability of sources means that 'the media often must attempt to communicate aspects of a complex situation in which certain interpretations are more easily rendered than others, regardless of the fairness and good faith of the journalist' (4).

Bell's report involves content analysis of the kind used in mine, counting how many times representatives of interested parties were interviewed in the programs, how often were they visually represented, how many times were direct sound bites used, and in the case of interviews on The 7.30 Report, how often was the interviewee challenged on matters of fact, their personal credibility, or just interrupted by the interviewer. In addition to these more empirical questions, the research also interpreted how the various interests in the dispute were labeled, how often success or failure was attributed to various interests, how responsibility for either outcome was attributed, and what metaphors and connotations were employed as a means of framing the representation of the dispute. In all of these more interpretive areas, Bell went much further than I had done in attempting to account for the way in which an issue was represented discursively rather than just in terms of the time allocated.

On the issues of balance and fairness, Bell's report found that there was an 'almost mathematical equivalence' in the number of sound bites from each side of the dispute (14) , and this was clearly the result of a highly professional attempt to present a balanced coverage of the events. The report also found that politicians were exposed to more challenging interviews, and were interrupted more often as they tried to put their points, than were other interviewees. However, as Bell pointed out, given that the bias of the program is to generate information for their audience, and given that politicians are responsible to that audience, that is not an unexpected finding nor an unreasonable expectation. He did note that the challenging interview was suffered by politicians from both sides of Parliament.

In response to the more interpretive issues – how the participants in the dispute were represented, the use of emotive or sensationalist language to frame the events or to attribute responsibility – Bell's report was much more cautious, warning that this is not an issue which can be 'adjudicated by objective means' (15). He did point out, though, that the use of emotive and conflictual strategies of representation was increasingly part and parcel of the way the news is presented today – and this was true for all providers. He then went on to suggest that the accusations of bias he was investigating may have proceeded from a distaste for precisely this kind of development – of increasingly tabloid or confrontational news and current affairs formats. (If that were so, mind you, one wonders why the ABC would be the first port of call.) Bell's concluding observation on what his findings demonstrated is interestingly phrased: '[I]t is possible to conclude that the programs acted professionally and fairly insofar as balance and accuracy can be judged' (15). Far from the ringing endorsement my report provided, although certainly enough to enable the ABC's media release to claim that the final report concluded there was 'no evidence of bias', and that the coverage was 'professional, fair and in line with journalistic norms and responsibilities' (27 July, 1998).

The fact that the Bell report carefully sidestepped drawing firm conclusions from its analysis of the programs' precise modes of visual and verbal representation may well have encouraged the kind of attack that was launched upon the ABC's coverage of the second Gulf War in 2003. That is, given that several reports had been able to disprove the more empirically based claims, Bell's circumspection suggested that there might be more mileage in focusing on those aspects that were not able to be 'adjudicated by objective means'.

That is more or less what Alston bowled up next. His list of 68 complaints was heavily weighted towards revealing the covert implication buried in the script, and the programmatic prosecution of a number of political 'themes' or points of view through such implications; this, rather than focusing upon formal indicators of balance. Murray Green's 130-page response, which constituted the ABC's official reply to Alston's complaints, did more than merely examine the programs in question. It compared the ABC reports with reports of the same events compiled by the BBC, the *Washington Post*, Reuters, and the *Guardian* as well as against the original audio tapes of the relevant press conferences from which the reports were generated.[17] It is a truly massive analysis which is fully informed by the conditions within which journalists work, and in particular those obtaining when filing reports from a war zone. Two of the complaints were upheld. Thwarted but not satisfied, Alston commissioned yet another assessment from outside the ABC, which found a handful more of his complaints were substantiated – still an embarrassing outcome. By now, there was no way one could explain Alston's behaviour as simply the expression of personal distaste for contemporary news formats or even the pursuit of political leverage; this had taken on the characteristics of a vendetta or an obsession.

There are now multiple levels of ABC media monitoring set up to service the residue of this obsession. For instance, since 1998 the ABC has engaged an external media monitoring company, Rehame, to monitor 'the share of voice' of each party in state, territory and federal elections. The 'share of voice' is an indication of the voice time allocated to federal members of parliament and party officials on ABC television, radio and online. The first pre-election monitoring report on the coverage of the 2004 federal election came out on 3 September, 2004, and it found that the share of voice between the Coalition government and the ALP had the government at 56.8 per cent and the ALP at 38.6 per cent on television. This was seen to 'fairly reflect the contrast between an incumbent government and a responding opposition'. After the election, the ABC's election coverage review committee reported the monitoring had revealed that 'ABC outlets provided the two main parties with an almost identical share of airtime during the six weeks before the election, with the Coalition scoring a 44.6 per cent share of voice compared with Labor's 43.5 per cent' (Simper, 2004).

And so on it goes, year after year, report after report, complaint after complaint, chasing the chimera of ABC bias, rooting the Marxists out of their basements, and hauling the 'lefties' at the ABC back into line. Now,

I'm not claiming that the ABC is without fault: of course, any media outlet which attempts to generate critical debate about public policy will have moments when opinion plays a larger role than it should and I am sure there have been many such occasions over the ABC's history. What I am responding to is the long history of disproved or discredited accusations and the implausible singularity of their focus upon the ABC, which also just happens to be the media organisation with the longest tradition of independent political journalism. While claiming the highest of motives and therefore (one would think) keen to encompass as much of the media as possible, the 'media bias' lobby completely ignores commercial television even though the majority of Australians get their news there. It is highly unlikely that political bias, whenever it occurred, would be unique to the ABC. However, the question of how the commercial media might be biased is virtually never raised. Perhaps such criticism would be pointless, even if there were those brave enough to generate it, given the commercial media's imperviousness to criticisms of their performance. Certainly, governments clearly believe that they have more influence over the ABC than they do over the commercial networks. Where governments are careful not to offend the major media organisations in case they provoke a response they cannot control, there is very little risk involved, these days, in bullying the ABC. Consequently, the fetish of ABC bias has become a handy strategy for governments of the day to harrry the national broadcaster so that it thinks twice before it presents stories that are critical of that government. To the extent that the ABC continues to present such stories, it is an admirably courageous organisation, but we shouldn't require quite that level of courage for it to perform its most valuable service for a democratic nation.

The liberal-democratic bias

All of that said, I need now to come at this from another angle. Debates about bias tend to take for granted the assumption that it is possible to strip representations of any bias – and that journalism should aspire towards the achievement of an absolutely pure objectivity. This, of course, is impossible. Stuart Hall reminded us, many years ago, that the media (in his case, the UK media) was in fact hopelessly biased: biased, that is, in favour of parliamentary democracy (Hall, 1982)... That is what we expect from it. Philip Bell's report makes a similar point when it rightly insists that the media should be biased in favour of its audiences; that is, biased towards critical scrutiny of the information provided to the public. The media's default position should be skeptical. Although journalism likes to argue that it must preserve objectivity as the foundation of its professional practice, the fact is that all re-presentations of events are going to proceed from an implicit point of view, whether it is sufficiently pronounced or divergent for us to notice it or not. Our own view of the world we will see as unproblematic; it is not a point of view, it is just the way things actually are. Therefore we regard a representation as objective if we can discern no gap between its viewpoint and our own; we attribute to it no point of view at all – it is transparently true. On the other hand, we receive a representation as biased when we do discern such a gap, and greater the gap the stronger the impression that this communication is advancing a particular point of view and is therefore biased.[18]

The points of view from which a communication may proceed do not have to be party-political. Indeed, they can be far less explicit than that. When we choose the newspaper we want to read or the television current affairs program we watch, we may do so because the view of the world we receive from those choices is largely consonant with our own. We may not think of that as a view of the world, however; we may just think that on most things this newspaper, or that program, gets it right. In Australia, the points of view taken in the print media certainly can be identified, but they are not usually presented to us as points of view; rather, they are implicitly endorsed as the right way to interpret events.

When, for instance, *The Australian*'s economics commentator Alan Wood presents us with his market-oriented account of government policy, there is nothing in what he says to indicate that the principles upon which his opinions are based are a source of bias. When Wood, and other conservative economic commentators, describe the market as an efficient means of distributing goods and opportunity, and recommend it as a more effective means of doing this than the government, they would be offended if this was described to them as an ideology. Even though there is no conclusive evidence to support this position and many would dispute it, and even though the belief in the efficacy of the market is an article of faith rather than something which is open to objective proof, there is nothing in the way Alan Wood presents his views which suggests that they should be regarded as in any way provisional. Within the Australian media overall, his kind of market-oriented economic and social philosophy has been in the ascendancy for some time – as it has in politics. What is good for the market, what is good for business, what is good for economic development – these are the objectives which have dominated the policy agenda for several decades. Therefore, those media outlets which align their points of view more or less with that orthodoxy may pass as presenting perfectly objective, unbiased reporting and analysis. What they are doing, nonetheless, is presenting a highly partisan market-economics-oriented view of the world that can easily misrepresent and misunderstand the events and histories upon which it is reporting. The Australian media's chronic incapacity to maintain independent scrutiny of the commercial and ethical behaviour of Australian business, from Bond Corp through to One.Tel, is enough to demonstrate this. Indeed, as I have argued elsewhere, the business press is so thoroughly in the capture of its sources that it is not at all surprising that it has proved unable to provide us with the independent information which might protect us from these high-profile corporate disasters.[19]

The ABC is increasingly the odd one out in this scenario. Its implicit point of view – 'bias', if you like – is towards a liberal-democratic view of the world which sees social policy as at least as important as economics, and which attempts to think about the effects of policy on more than just business – upon the everyday lives of the citizens, for instance. This 'bias' is implicit and not at all aggressive; it does not impinge on journalists' operation of their professional codes of balance and objectivity, but it is built into the orientation of how they understand and present news and current affairs. The ABC takes a critical view of the news in pursuit of clarifying the national interest. It has not always been alone in this endeavour. Its partner in the public sector, SBS, has also a long record of critical news and current affairs reporting through such programs as *Dateline* and *Insight*. Both the Nine and Seven networks have hosted programming that took a similar line in the past. Mike Willesee, for one, built his career in the commercial sector very much as a media crusader, taking on large issues and dealing particularly effectively with politicians. A Willesee interview in the 1970s and early 1980s was not an anodyne affair – and nor were those of his most effective successor, Jana Wendt. The

Nine Network's *Sunday* program has for many years presented investigative cover stories which employed a version of journalism that was not significantly different to that which generated *Four Corners*. Most recently, the Seven Network's *Witness* tried to revive that tradition – explicitly – by organising its format around one key investigative story each week and by naming itself as a 'public affairs' rather than a 'current affairs' program. However, as the trends I have been outlining in this book have developed, journalism that approached public affairs from this liberal-democratic point of view has declined. To a degree, it is reasonable for the commercial networks to leave that to the public broadcasters – they don't have the complications of commercial relationships and ratings figures to deal with. The extent to which this has occurred, though, is a cause for concern, particularly since the commercial orthodoxy is to deny that it has happened at all. 'Giving the public what it wants' is offered as the rationale, rather than 'not rocking the boat'. There are many consequences of this, and among them is the public broadcaster's increased vulnerability to criticism of its news and current affairs performance.

Ironically, while I argued earlier that there was an increase in the amount of pressure placed on the ABC under Alston's regime as minister, one would have to say that this doesn't seem to have been provoked by a particularly vigorous expression of the ABC's determination to remain independent, courageous, and critical of governments of the day. To the contrary, there is every reason to argue that Alston's pressure has had its effect and that a level of self-censorship and caution has crept into the day-to-day practices of producing news and current affairs within the network. Indeed, in an article for *The Australian* in November, 2004, former *Four Corners* executive producer and former head of ABC TV current affairs programs, Peter Reid, warned that 'a once-resolute spirit of inquiry and challenge in tackling contentious issues risks lapsing into inordinate caution and compliance' as a result of the continual monitoring of ABC content for political bias. Under threat, according to Reid, was 'public trust in the national broadcaster's editorial credibility' (2004: 18).

I mentioned in chapter 2 how struck I was by the confidence with which *TDT* countered accusations of bias in its 1000th episode; rather than attempting to defend themselves against such accusations the program proudly acknowledged that it took a point of view deliberately as a means of generating a strong and socially engaged story. Journalism with a point of view *was* defensible for the *TDT* producers and they backed the strength of the stories such journalism produced as the evidence of their professionalism and significance. Today, it seems that all the ABC can do is to try to keep a low profile so that it doesn't draw attention to itself; when that fails, it can commission an investigation in the vain hope of generating conclusive proof, or it can set up yet another monitoring mechanism to ward off accusations about any shifts in the balance of representation. The comparison is revealing. *TDT* gave no ground at all on the social value of a committed and principled journalism, while the contemporary ABC is just bent on survival on whatever terms can be negotiated with the bullies in Canberra. Interestingly, *TDT* took its position without the support of its management.

Running on empty

The place where all of this is visible, of course, is on the screen. In the ABC news bulletins, the merging of radio and television reports has cut the number of reporters but it has at least enabled the maintenance of a credible number of foreign correspondents. While journalists may not like the merged roles – understandably pointing to the different requirements of television and radio reporting – it does seem to be the way of the future. SBS's long-running[20] *Dateline*, itself probably the Australian program most experienced in providing quality international current affairs, has pioneered the use of the 'video-journalist', where individual operators are responsible for handling the commentary and video by themselves. The results are patchy, some complain about the amateurish quality of some stories, but it does generate some advantages – not only in terms of cutting costs but also in terms of flexibility, mobility and immediacy. Even with the cost-cutting measures, the ABC's international dimension is clearly the one most under strain and yet that is the area where my 1996 research found such conclusive evidence of the national importance of the ABC providing Australians with independent access to international news stories. The reduction in the number of Australian international correspondents working for the Nine Network has further magnified the differentials in the meantime, and there is reason to be concerned about Australians' access to our own sources of international news.

The day-to-day effect of Canberra's financial pressure upon the ABC is evident in the fact that there are insufficient funds for *The 7.30 Report* to present as many investigative stories per night as *TDT* did almost three decades ago – despite dramatic advances in production and communications technologies over that period. Instead *The 7.30 Report* has become the home of the dreaded 'two-way' – with the host interviewing a staff reporter or political correspondent about what they have found out from some third person. It is cheap, there is little alternative, but it places us at least three steps away from direct access to the source. There have been some flirtations with reconstructions over recent years, too, one of the markers of more tabloid approaches because of the highly dubious means through which the stories must be constructed. That is, to put the events on screen at all the producers must almost inevitably include material that is invented or assumed as well as that which is known. However, for me the most obvious problem is the disproportionate weight that has to be carried by the Kerry O'Brien interview, particularly the political ones. O'Brien is highly skilled and these days generates a wonderfully weather-beaten integrity. But there is very little for him to work with. There is rarely any evidence of the interview being informed by independent investigation and so the chances of interviewees ever being surprised by what is presented to them are virtually nil. Often there is no new information to inform the interview at all and so it becomes an entirely ritualised performance where the players each do what they have to do, and conclude when the time is up. Watching Kerry O'Brien interview Peter Costello on Budget night is like watching two cats attempt to play with the same mouse. The possibility of any new information emerging from the performance is very slim indeed and both participants seem to take solace in their enjoyment of their playing out of the ritual. Not only is this unproductive in terms of information, but it runs down the value of the interview as a genre of television performance. It is hard to remember, now, that such interviews could be entertaining, informative and even exciting. We are a long way from the disbelieving silence of a Willesee interview, from Ron Casey storming off the set rather than answer Jana Wendt's questions in front of a live audience, and from Richard Carleton sneering at Bob Hawke, 'How does it feel to have blood on your hands?' – all of them moments where contesting points of view that were of public importance were turned into dramatic and revealing television.

The formats in play, then, are cheap, defensible, but weary. The once-formidable ABC news and current affairs machine is now running on empty. When compared with what might be done – significantly, with what has been done in the past – its flagship programs are deeply unsatisfactory. I am aware that comments about funding affecting what is on screen are vulnerable to the criticism that this overlooks what happens internally – that is, the allocation of funds into news and current affairs is also subject to the internal politics of the ABC and they certainly seem to be, characteristically, both murky and deadly. That may be so, and others would be in a better position to assess this, but the external political vulnerability of news and current affairs cannot help in the internal battles for limited funds.

There are places in the ABC schedule where innovation and energy can be found, though, and where ratings are solid. In chapter 4, I mentioned the success Andrew Denton's evening talk show *Enough Rope* had found with a younger demographic who have turned off conventional current affairs, as well as its unexpected capacity to break news stories from time to time. The other program which deserves a mention in this context is *Australian Story*. *Australian Story* attracts an audience of around 1.3 million in a good week, a little better than the numbers pulled in by *Today Tonight* and *A Current Affair* each weeknight. Their format, which focuses on the stories of individuals, exposes them to accusations of merely performing an elevated version of celebrity journalism, but it is certainly more than that (see Bonner, 2003b). *Australian Story* is classified as current affairs; indeed, when I once left it off a published list of current affairs programs I was quickly reminded by the producer, Deb Fleming, that this is what it is. Running against the grain of the trend towards more sensationalist and confrontational formats, eschewing the use of a charismatic reporter to take us through the story (although it does have Caroline Jones to introduce most episodes), *Australian Story* deals with its subjects in a respectful and non-judgmental way, apparently allowing them the freedom to tell their story with the minimum of mediation. The interviewer is largely left out of the picture, their questions removed so that we have direct access to the subject – much in the way of *Attitude*, although with a less distinctive visual style. There is no challenging confrontation between reporter and subject, and the program's subjects are allowed to speak to the camera for relatively long periods of time.

I have heard it said that within the ABC there are those who are very critical of *Australian Story's* approach to current affairs journalism: for them, it is far too 'soft' and wastes the opportunity to put its subjects on the spot or to challenge their points of view. In some ways it is a rather old-fashioned format with its gentle editorial approach reminiscent of earlier ABC series such as *A Big Country*. Perhaps this is why it seems to have a slightly anomalous role within ABC news and current affairs, generating strong ratings but not winning the approval of core news and current affairs staff.[21] Yet, by giving their subjects 'enough rope' in the way they do, the producers of *Australian Story* have often created highly revealing, news-worthy, and multi-award-winning, television. The profile of Brisbane Broncos' coach Wayne Bennett displayed a dimension to his life that had been invisible until then, and was presented in a warm and appreciative manner that enabled it to work as a moving personal story. The profile of (then) ATSIC chair Geoff Clarke did not ask him the 'hard' questions, it is true, and in a way was all the more discomforting for that. What it did, though, was provide us with much needed background on the man and his family which helped contextualise his present situation, something that is smack dab in the middle of the traditional purpose of current affairs jour-nalism and, in this particular case, urgently needed. The program accom-plished this without confrontation, without oversimplifying the issues, and without telling the viewer what to think. In a final example, the episode which allowed the (then) Governor-General Peter Hollingworth to put his side of the story in response to charges that he had mishandled allegations of sexual abuse while in his former position, turned out to be politically explosive. This was not because he was worn down by the challenging interview, but because he was allowed to speak honestly for long enough to reveal the gap in his understanding of what would have been appropriate behaviour in the circumstances.

Australian Story might not look like *The 7.30 Report* or *Today Tonight*, but the stories it tells and the way it tells them are valid components of tele-vision current affairs formats. The fact that such an award-winning program, which rates highly, breaks news and generally does everything the network could reasonably expect, does not appear to have the unqualified admiration of its colleagues in ABC News and Current Affairs is a little worrying, and reflects some of the obstacles to generating new approaches to current affairs in today's ABC – and it is on this issue I want to conclude this chapter.

Let me go back to where we started: Laurie Oakes' provocative announcement that the Nine Network was now truly the national network. Reports subsequent to that announcement suggested that many senior ABC personnel were extremely concerned about it – and about the circumstances which had given the Nine Network the opportunity to make such a claim. Some felt that the decision not to screen the debate at the same time as the Nine Network was in fact a dereliction of one of the core responsibilities of the ABC's charter. This issue had come hot on the heels of the earlier decision made by the ABC's managing director, Russell Balding, not to break from normal programming in order to cross to a live broadcast of the Prime Minister's announcement of the 2004 federal election. Put together, both of them breaking with the precedents of many years, these two events seemed to signal a significant withdrawal from the ABC's news and current affairs responsibilities. In a feature for *The Australian* on the following weekend, Mark Day suggested that there was a corporate battle under way within the ABC, with news and current affairs firmly in the sights of the Director of Television, Sandra Levy:

> [S]he is known to be antipathetic towards the news and current affairs division and, in the view of some analysts, she is wrong to put a higher value on the needs and balance of her entertainment schedule than the demands of reporting the nation's significant events. (2004:21)

The burden of Day's piece was to suggest that the ABC was edging towards relinquishing its interest in its news and current affairs responsibilities, and that this was becoming easier as it became more successful in attracting ratings to its entertainment schedule. He quoted critics who foreshadowed the development of a new policy orientation at the ABC, under which the ABC withdrew 'from its core responsibility to report the nation to itself'. Alston's Mansfield agenda returns, only this time prosecuted from within.

There have been similar reports in relation to SBS TV as well. Changes in the management team over 2003–4 placed a new emphasis on the need for SBS to provide entertainment, and some high-profile departures indicated their discomfort with a shift which they regarded as a significant attack on the character and mission of SBS. With SBS already perched on the thin end of the wedge in that they do carry advertising, it would not be

hard to see it turn into something else quite quickly. Their budgetary constraints are even worse than those of the ABC, although they tend not to
come into conflict with government as often because of their primary
interest in providing international news and current affairs. However,
viewed together, the plight of the two public broadcasters would suggest
that their survival in their current forms is in danger: they face the twin
threats of a gradual commercialisation in the form of an increasing importance being given to ratings and to entertainment, and political pressure
from the government of the day.

If we put such possibilities against the scenario I have been outlining
throughout this chapter – of an ABC becoming increasingly cowed as a
result of government bullying and the pressure over funding – and the
observation one might make that much of the programming in news and
current affairs has run out of energy, then the prospects for the future are
not good. ABC news and current affairs is clearly embattled and that alone
is already dramatically inhibiting their willingness to take a point of view
on the events they report and analyse. It is hard not to regard the twin pressures produced by the bias lobby and the funding cuts as at the root of this
situation, and they have generated a situation that all Australians will ultimately regret. The national broadcaster is, *pace* Laurie Oakes, the one
which is funded by our taxes, and among its responsibilities must be the
provision of the kind of public good programming which the commercial
sector is unwilling to provide: at the moment, that happens to be committed, informed, investigative, high quality reporting on current affairs.
The political pressures exerted upon the ABC have been driven, largely, by
short-term political concerns with little interest in the long-term consequences; my argument in this chapter is that the long-term consequences
will be to reduce significantly the capacity and, ultimately, the will to
perform this essential service for the community.

NOTES

1   It was broadcast on Channel 9 on 12 September, and re-broadcast later that
     evening by Channel 2. The first screening was easily out-rated by a compilation of
     the worst contestants of the series *Australian Idol* on Channel 10.

2   The ABC's news and current affairs chief, John Cameron, was clearly miffed and
     responded as follows: 'Despite how Nine might try to paint themselves they're not
     the national broadcaster, the ABC is quite obviously the national broadcaster. And
     the ABC is not driven by unadulterated commercial interests, not to mention polit-
     ical affiliations. There's no other media organisation in the world, with the qualified

exception of the BBC, that has more than 50 newsrooms and radio stations dotted around the continent pumping out thousands of hours of local content a week. Nine and the other commercials don't come anywhere near that sort of coverage' (quoted in Meade, 2004: 24).

3   This comes from the ABC's report of the Newspoll on the ABC website (see the url at note 5, below).

4   *Sixty Minutes* has deliberately left it to others to provide context and analysis, instead focusing on the individual participants in an event and using their testimony as a means of dramatising the story rather than explaining it. Gerald Stone is famously reputed to have said that if *Sixty Minutes* was to do a story on the Great Flood, it would interview Noah.

5   Indeed, I was reminded of this by an extremely apposite press release that arrived as I was writing this piece. Headed 'Bias not an issue for the ABC', and published on 3 September, 2004, the release quotes a Newspoll of community attitudes to the ABC which 'continues to confirm that the Australian public overwhelming (sic) believe that the ABC is "balanced and evenhanded" in its reporting of news and current affairs. Recent monitoring of ABC output by Rehame in the lead up to the federal Election also supports the ABC's standing as an independent and impartial public broadcaster' (<http://www.abc.net.au/corp/pubs/s1191509.htm>. Accessed 4.9.2004).

6   When Richardson left federal politics, he took up a position with Kerry Packer.

7   Well, that's not quite true. I did find one extremely anomalous report of allegations of political bias at Channel 9 in Brisbane, from 1985 (see Sweetapple, 1985: 2).

8   This was the result of *Today Tonight* screening a report from Spain which deliberately misrepresented the location of the reporter as being in Majorca while he was filmed driving through the streets of Barcelona.

9   Shipp, 1971: 26–23; see also Gibbons, 1971: 90–96; and Shipp and Tiffen, 1991: 19–26.

10 See McAdam 1983: 53–61; Harris, 1985: 10.

11 This is a point reinforced by Rod Tiffen's criticism that discussions of bias rarely 'take seriously the news media as institutions with their own routines, constraints, incentives and traditions' (2000: 191), which, he implies, stand in the way of a simple notion of media bias.

12 Henningham, 1982: 74–75. This research eventually comprised Henningham's PhD thesis, 'Australian television journalists' professional values and audience orientations' (University of Queensland, 1984); and a subsequent development from this project was also published (see Henningham, 1995: 321–334).

13 It is probably worth making the gratuitous observation here that it is a little rich for anyone in the Murdoch press to be accusing others of editorial bias. The *Walkley Magazine* has pointed out that all 175 of the Murdoch press outlets worldwide took a pro-war position during the Iraq war: 'a somewhat surprising statistic ... given that in countries such as Australia and the UK the population was roughly divided on the issue' (Malone, 2003: 16).

14 That is, it tended to pick up stories that had been generated in-house, were not

news in any sense at all, but which would provide a highly promotable story for thenetwork. Hidden camera stories, celebrity interviews and the range of topics we have already identified with the sprint downmarket are what I was counting.

15　Turner 1996a: 140. This is the published form of the report, and all the percentages and other data referred to in the above paragraph are drawn from it (1996a: 127–65). It contains the full tables outlining the research outcomes and so gives a great deal more detail than I can go into here. There were some typographical errors in this article when it was first published and they were corrected subsequently (Turner, 1997: 171-2).

16　Philip Bell: 'ABC News, the 7.30 Report and the "Waterfront Dispute(s)" April–May 1998', <http://www.abc.net.au/corp/pubs/bell1.pdf>.

17　This report can be found on the ABC's reports website, <http://www.abc.net.au/corp/pubs>.

18　Tiffen makes the point that conventional understandings assume that media representation has its greatest impact when it is most biased, but that this misunderstands the processes I have been outlining. It is not necessarily the case, he says, that news coverage has most impact when it is most biased. Indeed, the reverse would seem to be true: that once bias is evident, the capacity for it to influence understandings must be reduced (2000: 191).

19　In my 1994 book, *Making it National*, I outlined how the media were complicit in the rise of Alan Bond, and the structural connections between journalists and their corporate sources.

20　It celebrated its 20th year in 2004.

21　Bonner (2003b) argues that one of the reasons for its anomalous placement within the ABC is that it is produced in Brisbane and has inherited a special remit for rural coverage. She points to its hybrid format, mixing current affairs and documentary, as well.

CHAPTER SIX

Other sources of news and current affairs: pay TV and the Internet

Introduction

In this chapter, I want to move beyond the free-to-air networks. The first section will focus on pay-TV news and current affairs, in particular upon CNN. In the second section, responding to what many see as the coming competitor to television news and current affairs, I will turn to the opportunities offered by news services on the Internet, opportunities that many would argue will turn out to be decisive because of their capacity to change the way we make and consume news.

The first section of the chapter is a reflection of some of my thoughts when pay TV was introduced to Australia as it documents my response to my own 'first contact', as I call it, with the pay-TV news services, Sky and CNN, in 1997.[1] In particular, it focuses upon my thoughts at the time about the potential for pay-TV news to change the news landscape in Australia, and to contribute to local and national debates at that time – and as such, it probably comes closer to a form of 'testimony' than cultural analysis. Then, at the end of this section, I want to consider the present situation: the kinds of contributions pay TV is making today.

Most academic discussions of Australian broadcast television – and there are not that many[2] – have focused, in one way or another, on the relationship between television and national culture. The introduction of pay

TV has complicated this relationship, but the take-up has been slow and the programming genres are still quite limited, and pay TV does not yet play a major role in generating the talk, gossip and debate that is so much a part of the pervasiveness of broadcast television's contribution to what John Hartley calls 'popular reality' – a popular media culture. It is not surprising, therefore, that virtually all discussion of pay TV in Australia has been at the level of policy, particularly regulation and ownership. As a consequence, we have focused on policy outcomes rather than on new programming strategies or on the introduction of a new regime of media consumption. There has been little attempt, so far, to see what kind of contribution pay TV makes to our news and current affairs diet, how it alters our patterns of consumption, or influences our view of our place in the world. This is my response, then, to an alternative source of news drawn from my own 'first contact' with pay TV and, more specifically, with CNN.

First contact

The scene must have been repeated all the way down the street. Optus had just finished putting up its cables and was now peddling an introductory trial offer: installation and one month's rental free, no obligations. The Optus cable guy, who was young and dressed for an active day in shorts, runners and an Optus baseball cap, was more persistent than persuasive but we signed up anyway. I had a professional interest, after all. Mind you, I had always thought that the Australian market could not sustain competition in pay TV, and that the likely loser in the battle would be Optus. But, as the cable guy said, they had the Disney channel, MTV, and both Sky News and CNN ...

Of course, it was not that novel or exciting. Like many other Australians, I had spent time in overseas hotels testing the Bruce Springsteen thesis – '57 channels and nothing on' – and found that it mostly held up. For me, seated in a hotel room in the US at various points during the early 1990s, watching television became the watching of segments, just like the television theorist John Ellis says (1982), rather than watching whole programs. We can all probably recall our first encounters with the remote control and a pay-TV schedule. The possibility that something 'better' might have started on another channel in the last five minutes seems to drive the viewer through the full range of systematically mediocre programming, exercising choice way past the point where it is likely to deliver either surprise or satisfaction. Rather than finding one's hold on the distinctions between programs slipping, as in Raymond Williams' famous experience in the Miami hotel room where all the programs seemed to be happening to him at once (1974: 92), the sensation is one of neurotic enervation; pleasure is deferred and then bathetically denied as an hour passes and you have actually 'watched' nothing but the performance of television's delivery of choice. This, I admit, may well turn out to have been a generation- and culture-specific observation; years ago, some American students of mine kindly took me aside to tell me that watching television is something you can only do properly with a remote control, and without my generation's anxieties about narrative closure. Be that as it may, I have always found watching television like this an especially unsatisfying experience. Ken Wark has noted one curious by-product of such a state of mind. The pervasive 'Americanness' of the pay-TV programming has a slightly consoling effect: it ends up holding the programs together, 'stabilising the flow of meanings'.[3]

It was different in my living room. At first, the greatest benefit of pay TV in my living room was the fact that I could finally get perfect reception on free-to-air! The movies (three channels) asked more of me than I was prepared to give to television most of the time; the sound of the cartoon channel in the next room set my teeth on edge and most of my favourite sports were 'live' at two in the morning. I did, though, put real effort into getting to know my news channels. At first glance, they were disappointing. Sky's Australian News was, as it is now, totally dependent upon its free-to-air sources, much of the hourly headline updates already broadcast word-for-word, shot-for-shot, on the commercial networks; other local content, as it does now, mostly consisted of time-shifted broadcast programs such as *Today, Sunday, Today Tonight* and so on. The repetitiousness of the basic bulletin formats used by Sky News and CNN means that they cannot be used in the same way as broadcast news, where whole bulletins are screened at times that punctuate the routines of the day. For Australian consumers, unlike the American viewer of CNN or the British viewer of Sky, these bulletins are not grounded in a time zone, a daily rhythm of work or leisure time, or indeed in a clear sense of place. CNN, at times, seems to disavow any spatial location at all; so, rather than creating a 'virtual geography', its projected ubiquity seems to displace geography altogether.

The world of news CNN constructs is significantly different from free-to-air. Operating in a virtual space makes it quite an abstract experience – implicitly homogeneous and timeless, and inherently spectacular rather than meaningful. The process of newsgathering is turned into a performance of technology and corporate organisation that is always poised on the brink of self-congratulation. I found that CNN did have some novel ideas, though. The *Q&A* segment which brought guests into the studio for a current affairs interview that is accomplished through viewer questions sent by fax, letter, or email, had a whiff of possibility, but its brevity kept it tame and anodyne. More interesting was the 6.30 pm news review for kids, *CNN: Newsroom*, which definitely suggested how network news might address a younger audience without becoming tame, anodyne or patronising. It was not these features of programming content, however, which came to interest me in my living room. Rather, as these features were assimilated into my daily viewing behaviour, it became clear that consuming CNN on study leave in a hotel in Chicago was very different to having your everyday consumption of CNN shape your access to sudden and important events – such as, for instance, the 1997 election of Tony Blair. To talk about this, I need to review some of the ways in which CNN differs from Australian broadcast television news and current affairs.

CNN, just like free-to-air news and current affairs services, has a vigorous interest in processing its information in the house style, and imposing a clear shape and order on the vast amount of material available for transformation. It has to do this, though, in ways that are very different from free-to-air. It does not promote its personalities as the primary marketing move, nor does it – nor can it – locate the significance of its content in relation to the viewer's identification with their own local, regional, or national concerns. Whereas our free-to-air services still legitimate themselves as services through extensive reference to the local, regional and national market and through the news-reading personality's address to the local or national viewer, CNN has to depend on its global reach, its imputed capacity to offer more detail, more background, more access than is possible within a commercial entertainment network. Despite the rhetorical power of the notion of globalisation, we know that CNN has had to adapt to the demands of regional markets and now offers slightly differentiated services and new specialised programs in order to compete. Further, whereas it would be fair to say that free-to-air networks promote their personalities more vigorously than their news values, the globalised character of CNN's corporate image demands a sort of anonymity – a generic corporate professionalism – from its anchors and reporters. A positive conclusion could be drawn from this comparison. Unlike the Australian free-to-air commercial networks, CNN actually has to depend on its content – on its capacity to deliver an informative news service, be it ever so homogenised and bite-sized, to an audience that is most probably looking for news before entertainment.

In common with the American free-to-air networks, CNN uses its narrow range of programming genres to differentiate between 'hard' and 'soft' news, between political news and lifestyle programming and so on. It is the blurring of such distinctions that provoked the contemporary criticism of Australian free-to-air news and current affairs we have considered throughout this book. Such terms as 'soft' news, 'lifestyle' programming, and our old friend 'tabloidism' refer us to programs on Australian commercial television where the personality of the host has been increasingly foregrounded. We have already seen how the trajectory that takes *A Current Affair* from trading on Michael Willesee's original status as a crusading investigative reporter, to Jana Wendt's potent mixture of independent professionalism and an iconic stardom, and then finally to Ray Martin's bloke-next-door interpellating[4] twinkle, accompanies a decline in the importance of the performance of journalism. With CNN, we are spared Ray's dimples and the cosily complicit relationship we are contracted to enjoy when we watch *A Current Affair*. Or, not to get carried away by the momentum of this comparison, if we are invited to respond to the CNN hosts in a similar way, the fact of their being on CNN provides the Australian viewer with a kind of licensed exemption from interpellation. I suspect that, no matter how familiar it becomes to Australian viewers, there may be a fundamental provisionality in our viewing relation to CNN. We 'watch' it with an ideological circumspection that comes from an ironic recognition of its 'foreignness' and of the need for sceptical readings of almost everything it says.

The current state of news and current affairs on Australian television, of course, probably makes CNN look better than it should. However, there is more to the comparison than that. There are significant, potentially progressive, differences in form and effect. As Wark suggests, what is best about CNN is its coverage of sudden, 'live' events. The live event coverage offers very different prospects to the viewer than those provided by the repetitive headline formats; in the former, the viewer is suddenly brought into alignment with what Wark describes as a 'form of abstract news time' (1994: 39). The viewer's experience of this 'news time' feels anything but abstract, I'd suggest, and among the reasons for this is the formal distinctiveness of the CNN format Wark describes:

> Being a twenty-four hours news service, it does not have the luxury of collecting evidence of an event for hours before the nightly newscast and compressing the available data into conventional journalistic and narrative form. CNN has introduced the queer concept of 'live' news coverage – an instant audiovisual presence on the site of an event. Consequently, CNN reports frequently lack focus and narrative direction. In seeking to speed up the audiovisual news vector, the station has dispensed as much as possible with the narrative strategies of American network news practice, if not its visual conventions. It has also dispensed with expensive, authoritative anchorpersons. In a news strategy based on pure speed, which increases the possibility for error, the Dan Rather style of narrator really has no place. (38)

The result can be the opposite of the decontextualised sound bite which typifies free-to-air strategies.

The potential carried by the CNN format was impressed on me, over the period of my 'first contact', while watching its coverage of the British election in 1997. CNN covered much of the election 'live'. Once the result was known, CNN focussed on the moments when defeat was conceded and victory claimed, including some moments of kitsch political pageantry (the visit to the Queen) before moving to wait outside 10 Downing Street for the new Prime Minister to take possession. This was an historic moment, of course, but lower down the scale than the 'global media events' Wark covers in *Virtual Geography*: the Gulf War, the Tienanmen Square massacre, and the Wall Street crash. Indeed, crucial to my interest here is how undramatic much of the footage actually was. The cameras waiting outside endured long periods when very little happened. Confronting the dilemma faced by the sports commentator covering a match in which the result is clear well before the end, the journalists had to find secondary items of interest to focus on and moved from analyst to analyst, offering a range of contextual briefings. These were repetitive and increasingly spec- ulative in content. Boredom hovered, but I was struck by how effectively this was countervailed by the drama generated solely through the spectac- ular immediacy, the 'live'-ness of the coverage. While, on the one hand, this is probably a consequence of CNN's fundamental commitment to the display of its technological capacity, on the other hand, the doggedness with which the live coverage was maintained in defiance of the patent lack of exciting footage could also be regarded as a sign of the network's com- mitment to news, rather than entertainment, values. What struck me about it most, however – what indicated that this was a slightly different regime of television production to what I was used to – was that it constituted a routine and strategic renunciation of television's capacity to process and transform its material into shapely and coherent programming.

The results, from time to time, were both entertaining and interesting. The Labour victory was clearly an exceptional event, and as a Labor voter seated in Howard's benighted battler's paradise in 1997 it was impossible not to watch with a longing avidity. When Blair turned up at Downing Street, he and his wife proceeded to shake hands with the whole crowd. Thousands had turned up to line the street in welcome. CNN simply fol- lowed the pair up and down the street as they performed this ritual, without cutting away and without a great deal of comment. Once it was complete, we watched as the photographers got their shots: some with the children, some without, some with Cherie hugging the new PM, some a little more formal, and so on. The speech, when it came, occurred with the barest attention to notes and helped provide a hint of narrative closure to what had been an extended period of uninterrupted live coverage.

The spectacular nature of CNN's performance of newsgathering is im- possible to ignore. As September 11 chillingly demonstrated, it is a remark- able experience to watch significant global events unfold 'live' on television. In this case, however, there was something else that interested me: the fact that we were receiving footage which was visually dull (it had the minimum amount of vision editing), poorly structured, repetitive and predictable in content, and at times plainly unwieldy for the reporters given the task of transforming it into news. As a result, it seemed to have moved slightly beyond the reach of the discursive conventions of television news. It was the raw material from which later bulletins would be produced, of course, but watching it gave me a sense of having moved a little closer to the process of definition, selection and transformation the discourses of television news have been developed to erase and disavow. Just a hint, mind you, but it felt as if someone had administered the antidote.

Heresy, perhaps, given most people's view of CNN. Outside the USA, CNN is widely regarded as the prime example of the political costs of a globalising media market and as a good reason to maintain local alternatives. Along with McDonalds and IBM, CNN has come to stand for a specifically American neo-imperialism of the kind implicit in the title of Daniel Hallin's discussion of American news media, borrowed from the 1985 CBS promotional slogan, 'We keep America on top of the world'.[5] CNN was accused of a disreputable complicity with the American military during the first Gulf War, and of engaging in an irresponsible commodification of the war as a spectacle for its viewers; Douglas Kellner's description is representative of such a view:

> The Gulf War was packaged as an aesthetic spectacle, with CNN utilizing powerful drum music to introduce their news segments, superimposing images of the US flag over American troops, and employing upbeat martial music between breaks. The audience was thus invited to participate in a dazzling war spectacle by its media presentations. (1995: 179)

In Australia, viewers resisted the gung-ho approach taken by CNN journalists being beamed twenty-four hours a day onto free-to-air channels, and turned to the ABC's coverage in unprecedented numbers. Since then, of course, we have seen much worse – the Fox News treatment of the second Gulf War and the effect which the practice of embedding journalists in combat units had upon the independence of their points of view. Nonetheless, even Hallin's hard-nosed critique of American news media practice places CNN as among the remaining hopes for 'serious journalism' in his country and notes the low-budget nature of the CNN operation – something that runs against the grain of the mythology of globalisation. And while CNN's audience reach may be substantial when considered as a global figure, its reach within specific national markets is actually minute.

Along similar lines, I was surprised by my sense of the positive potential accessible through these pay-TV news services within the Australian context. Maybe, here, the 'first contact' metaphor of this section's sub-heading comes into play. There is a shock at the apprehension of possibility implicit in this notion of 'first contact': the primitive or innocent response to something never encountered before but which immediately restructures the possibilities contained within our view of the world. I was surprised by the way in which CNN, and to a lesser extent the international aspects of Sky News programming, became part of my television viewing – even on days when the British government was not changing hands. I cruised past Sky and CNN, looking to see what it was they could provide me access to, today. With Sky World News, the fact that this was the British morning news replayed at prime time in the evening in Australia produced a slightly exotic effect; consuming the UK's daily, everyday programming, with the exploring, detached, gaze of the outsider has its attraction. A sturdy defender of local content, and of the need for television (especially news) to be grounded in the local/national, I had underestimated the pleasures of access, the metropolitanising buzz many of us experienced when first introduced to the Internet, and which comes from the use of new points of entry to information. This pleasure was enhanced and specified by the occasional, empowering possibility of seeing the raw footage that goes into the making of our free-to-air bulletins.

It is still the case, as it was back in 1997, that most of the programming on Sky World News and CNN seems unaware that anybody from Australia is watching. It doesn't even need to bother about 'colonising' the Australian viewer. The implications of that are insulting, perhaps, but it does have another effect on how we consume news delivered in this way. The programs are not only news from 'elsewhere' but they are, at times, presented unself-consciously in the discourses of that 'elsewhere' too: explicitly constructing forms of identification from which we are implicitly exempt (try watching Test cricket on Sky, for instance!). At such points, the program is doubly de-centred for the Australian viewer so that its qualities as a kind of text – not just the information it carries – become of direct interest and engaging with them becomes a central pleasure for the viewer. When the subject matter of such programs happens to be Australian (rare, but it happens, and more often on the international bulletins on Sky than on CNN), it becomes even more interesting – again, because the point of view is from a neo-colonial 'elsewhere'. In the case of these cable news services, then, watching how we are represented becomes an explicit attraction for the Australian viewer in ways that are not replicated when watching national broadcast bulletins.

Of course, and on balance, 'first contact' rarely works to the advantage of the 'Indigene' (if I can appropriate the metaphor in this way). Attractive though the contact may be to the local inhabitants, it is their domestic culture which is penetrated, modified and commodified through exposure to the representatives of another culture. We are still at the first stage of this process here. The crucial political point, after contact is made, is when the local culture sees how it is represented by the newcomers. CNN almost never speaks to us about Australia and it certainly never addresses an Australian viewer. If it could come to do that progressively, then it might have a genuinely important, although still very restricted, contribution to make to Australian political and popular culture. For the moment, though, we can say that it does offer access to alternative (extensive) sources of information, and occasionally the liberating sense of being able to bypass the conventional processes of news production in its depiction of live events. In the current context, this is a useful contribution to make – and more than I expected to gain from that encounter with the cable guy. It's still a pretty modest claim, however, to proceed from what is an admittedly personalised account of some changes in (my) viewing behaviour resulting from the connection of pay TV.

The claim probably has to remain fairly modest. In terms of the provision of news and current affairs programming in Australia today, the major influence from pay TV has been through the twenty four hour news services. A certain amount of hybrid programming of the type discussed in chapter 4 has developed: the trashy combination of news, opinion and sensationalism that marks Fox News, the youth-oriented talk and comedy formats found in Arena, for instance, the gender issues talk show *Mars Venus* on the W channel, or the combination of standard network current affairs and television talkback in Terry Willesee's *Willesee Across Australia*. Pay comes into its own when there is important news breaking live, but these days the free-to-air networks almost routinely depart from their schedules under such circumstances (as they did on September 11, for instance) in order to take up the service provided by CNN or BBC World. At such moments, aware as they are of the competition pay TV can generate, the free-to-air providers simply block the opposition. Nonetheless, the point I made in this earlier discussion, that the pay-TV news formats address the consumer of news, not the consumer of entertainment, remains true and they do constitute somewhere else for that consumer to go if they are disenchanted with what is offered on the free-to-air networks. The problem with that, of course, is that this is really only true of international news; for Australian material, even the pay services remain utterly dependent on the provision of material from free-to-air.

More so with current affairs. Very little current affairs programming dealing with Australian material is available exclusively on pay. Some years ago, when its influence was fresh, the decline of localism was often cited as one of the failings in network current affairs. While we may have become used to this, it would suggest that pay TV should face even stronger resistance if it is unable to generate significant national, let alone local, programming. Further, even though pay TV does provide us with access to some different formats for the discussion of global (or, mostly, American) current affairs – the Larry King program, for instance – these are not any more adventurous or diverse than those provided, say, by the SBS schedule (where we might pick up, say, the PBS's Jim Lehrer). The arrival of digital pay services does hold considerable potential for improving this situation, however. During the 2004 federal election, Sky News provided a dedicated election channel, with five separate screens assigned to the election on the night. In addition, they scheduled a regular current affairs program, *Election 2004*, at 9.30 pm seven days a week for the duration of the campaign, which interviewed candidates and provided comment and analysis, including a special segment from the Canberra press gallery on Monday nights. At the time, of course, only a limited number of viewers had access to these programs – around 500 000 households nationally – but it does indicate the potential for a multi-channel service that addresses its news agenda aggressively and aims squarely at a news audience.

Pay TV is still in the process of becoming embedded into a very specific system of 'popular reality' in Australia, with its national news networks for television and radio, the highly concentrated ownership of the print and electronic media, and the prominence of discourses of national identity, still, in all forms of local television programming and marketing. Further, pay TV does not look likely to displace the free-to-air networks as the major source of news and other programming any time soon; the prevailing features of the broadcast media climate continue to frame the context within which pay TV will be consumed. Among these features of the contemporary climate is its history of vigorous (if not uncontested) support for Australian sovereignty over the electronic and print media. The news services on CNN and Sky must operate in an oblique and highly mediated relation to such a climate and thus are, in general, hooked up to personal and cultural patterns of consumption far more tightly than to constructions of national or local identity. It is not, as the most simplified versions of the narrative of a globalising, postmodern media woud have it, that the introduction of pay TV and its burden of overwhelmingly American content necessarily will have a predictable and oppressive effect on the Australian mediascape, or on the relation between media consumption in Australia and the politics of identity. The process is much more complicated than that.

On the one hand, broadcast television as a form encourages the kind of 'sympathetic' identification[6] which privileges the familiar and 'the real' and which must reinforce the appeal of local broadcast television against the challenge of 'foreign' cable television – no matter how compelling the moments of 'liveness' CNN manufactures. On the other hand, there are attractive possibilities offered by pay TV which are almost entirely absent from the current range of broadcast television in Australia. Their attraction, however, produces a mode of consumption which, from my experience, would benefit from closer inspection. The hint of the cosmopolitan and the exotic generated by the news services I have been talking about occurs in conjunction and in competition with (at the very least) an essentially ironic modality of identification, motivated by our sense of exemption from CNN's interpellating discourses (such as they are) as well as the reflex and unpredictable operation of an historically ambivalent response to American influence. How this will play out as a means of identification for the Australian consumer of pay TV over time is difficult to predict, but there may be new modes of identification on offer which are not simply those implied by the grand narratives of globalisation or of omnivorous postmodern consumption.

While there is potential for significant change, then, I would still hold the position that broadcast news and current affairs will continue to frame political and other debates in Australia (and about Australia) for a long time to come. That has to be a worry, really, when we know how anodyne, how unadventurous, and how cynical the prevailing patterns of mainstream newsgathering have become. There are some other sources, however, many of which define themselves in opposition precisely to that kind of situation – as places where independent journalism may still flourish without fear of being beaten by the ratings or the sales figures. By and large, these sources are found on the Internet.

The alternative of online journalism

In a report commissioned by the Australian Broadcasting Authority (ABA) into the sources of news and current affairs in 2001, the authors, Jeff Brand and Mark Pearson, suggested that 'the tripartite relationship among audiences, providers and content of news and current affairs' was changing in Australia. They pointed out that the nature and direction of this trans-formation had complex determinants. On the one hand, they suggested that audiences and providers have turned away from what they described as 'hard news' but, on the other hand, the 'recent formulation of question-able current affairs content' has not provided what they are seeking. As a result, they continued, 'both audience and industry are seeking a new formula, one that will meet the needs of public policy and public good; and no doubt, one that will enrich the news and current affairs organisation that introduces and dominates it'.[7] Brand and Pearson pointed out that a larger number of Australians use the Internet for news and current affairs than use pay TV (the gap has grown larger in the meantime), and therefore it was not surprising that the Internet is one of the locations where many believe such a formula is being developed. In this section, I want to examine this possibility by discussing what is there at present, and what future directions seem reasonable to predict.

First, what is there at the moment? The answer to that must distin-guish between a number of different kinds of sites: at the very least, between the DIY-styled sites set up by individuals or small grassroots, often activist, organisations as alternatives to the mainstream mass media, and those established as part of an integrated corporate multiplatform strategy by existing mainstream media organisations.

The DIY or alternative sites tend to be networked, and to explain their rationale in terms of providing a richer, less commercially oriented, news diet than that offered by the mainstream media. As an example, the World Alternate News Network (*WANNet*) sets itself up in opposition to the 'Establishment Press by inviting the contribution of volunteers to generate 'the news you just don't see' (which is how they put it on their homepage). Their website argues that people want news that is independent of business: what they describe as the 'unfiltered truth'. This desire, they suggest, is 'more attainable today than it has ever been' because of the existence of the Internet. Breaking down the hierarchies which separate journalists from their readers, WANNet invites the participation of subscribers and contributors – whether 'they are an originator, conveyor or reader of news'. Although there is clearly a connection between this network and certain activist causes – the webpage from which I am quoting at the moment, for instance, was connected to anti-whaling activism[8] – the rules for contributors are very explicit about excluding the submission of opinion or comment: the list insists that it wants to provide news. Not all alternative news sites are like this, however, and many do foreground commentary, discussion and opinion as well as providing links to alternative sources of factual information.

Academic Axel Bruns describes the key attribute of these collaborative news networks in the following way. '[They] introduce fundamental changes to the very production of news reports', he says: 'rather than merely *adding* some representation of reader views in a contained area, they *replace* journalists with users in the role of content providers' (2004:181). On such sites (the examples he gives includes *Slashdot*, *Kuro5hini* and the sites of the Indymedia network), users themselves are encouraged to submit articles:

> Frequently, such articles serve as pointers to news material published elsewhere on the web, giving a brief summary of the information available and discussing its implications. They also provide a starting point for a communal discussion of that particular news report, and debate functions are usually directly attached to each published article for this purpose. (181)

These sites, Bruns suggests, are responding to the perceived shortcomings of mainstream news media by removing the function of the editor and the journalist in favour of expanding the role of the active and intelligent participant/consumer. All submissions are published, but are also open to comment, debate and revision: 'In Indymedia and similar sites, then, this making of newmedia (news) is inherently collaborative; news coverage is arrived at through conversation and dialogue rather than the traditional monologue of journalistic reporting' (185). The vibewire news site, *electionTracker.net*, which was set up during the 2004 election campaign, published articles written by regular contributors, employed editors and picture editors, but also provided the opportunity for subscribers to comment on every story published as well as to contribute to blogs and forums. The mix of election news was targeted at a young market, the personnel listed on their site were largely young journalism or media graduates,[9] and the site explicitly addressed its readers as sources of news and contributions – not only as consumers. Such strategies are consistent with approaches to the Internet that see it as common territory, analogous to the ancient property concept of 'the commons': a domain that was preserved for public use. The 'digital commons' finds one of its expressions through these alternative media sites and networks.[10]

There are problems with this, of course, idealistic as it is. As media academic Terry Flew reminds us, the Internet is the 'ultimate vanity press' (2002: 99) and it is afflicted with some of the same problems as the non-virtual version: the quality of editorial control, its capture by personal preferences and agendas, the ethics which guide publishing practices, and the issue of authenticating the status of the evidence it presents. The open access the Internet provides is both its benefit and its curse. One of the more recent practices to develop on the web, weblogging, would appear to be among the most self-indulgent publishing practices available. Weblogging involves maintaining an online diary which carries date-stamped messages in chronological order; 'blogs' can be hosted by individuals or collaboratively by groups and are noted for their 'individualistic and exhibitionistic style' (see Redden, 2003: 153–165). Blogging tends to be focused on commentary upon news, usually from the position of advocacy, rather than upon the attempt to generate new information or access to alternative news sources. As a result, bloggers are not known for checking their facts, or indeed for exhibiting much concern about that kind of reliability at all. Initially of little interest outside the Internet communities which developed them, weblogs suddenly leapt to public prominence during the second Gulf War. Then, as I mentioned earlier, the access of war correspondents was tightly controlled, in part by 'embedding' journalists into combat units – a process that effectively encouraged the alignment of journalists with the strategic objectives pursued by these units. Or, as researcher Guy Redden has put it, the tactic swiftly diverted attention 'from the case for or against war to its execution' (157). Much discussion has focused on how particular news networks behaved under these conditions and the whole exercise was tainted by its clear failure to generate sources of information which were independent of the military or of their political masters. Most particularly, it provided very little prospect of hearing from those most directly affected by the invasion – the citizens of Iraq. Within such a context, the publishing of weblogs from the war-zone assumed some political importance and attracted mainstream news media interest.

According to Redden's account, 'bloggers of the war produced a huge volume of material that encompassed a range of positions and topics' (158). Many used the blog as a means of disseminating information that was otherwise unpublishable: journalists or military personnel, for instance, did this. Other blogs were primarily opinion or analysis, delivered with varying levels of expertise; even more were personal testimonies giving voice to those experiences the mainstream media had proved unwilling or unable to access. Ironically, it was the failure of the mainstream media to extricate itself from the political agendas of the 'coalition of the willing' in order to develop independent sources of information that made the bloggers necessary, and that constructed a receptive audience for their testimony. Possibly the most famous warblogger was the Baghad architect, Salam Pax, who logged on regularly to provide eyewitness reports on the bombing of his city. Not content with simply providing his testimony about what was actually happening during this period, he also provided commentary and analysis – much of it scathing in its indictment of both the fallen Hussein regime and of the American invaders. Pax proved a skilled and effective polemicist, and his weblog was widely read and reported, exerting an influence on mainstream political debates about the conduct of the war.

The Gulf War bloggers generated new sources of news and current affairs – both fact and comment – and, as such, constituted a significant intervention into the international news economy. Redden suggests that this was their primary objective: to mediate between the standard news media and their audiences in terms of providing new content but more importantly in terms of providing an analysis of how political bias or spin was being played out in a context where they had first-hand access to information. In this regard, he notes, 'it is important to note that most warblogging, as a popular activity, depends upon a re-mediation of mainstream media content'. That is, he goes on to say, 'the personal slants that together amount to a new form of public discussion depend upon the existence of a professional media with privileged access to physical events and to primary sources'. Therefore, he differentiates himself from the more idealistic constructions of the Internet's alternative news sites by pointing out that the bloggers seize upon existing stories and work upon them, rather than 'creating an altogether alternative sphere of news and views' (162). As a result, he talks of the bloggers as 'new intermediaries' adding their voice to the media mix and invigorating public debate. However dependent they might be upon the news media which feeds them their material, he concludes that they constitute a means of 'allowing citizens' voices to carry in ways that they have not done before' (163).

It is important to acknowledge that not all alternative news sites have this kind of pro-social objective, however. For example, the multitude of celebrity news sites, cosily located next to soft porn sites in most cases, are not about providing an alternative: they simply repurpose (re-package for a different purpose) and redistribute existing material – photos, videos, reports lifted from the press and so on. We also have the Internet scandal sheet typified by the US *Drudge Report*, which depends upon the notoriety it has developed for its blend of tabloid political and entertainment industry gossip and scandal. Matt Drudge, the site's proprietor, aims for impact, primarily, and his site is free of any manifesto or set of principles which might set him up as an advocate for a more independent media. Instead, he stands in the long tradition of the US 'yellow press'. The 'digital commons' has more than its share of muck-rakers.

To move away from these minority or alternative locations, by far the most important influence on news and current affairs information on the web remains the usual suspects: the established media organisations. These are still the dominant feature of the mediascape online, despite the free-Internet rhetoric. Surveys of hit-rates routinely indicate that it is the online presence of mainstream media organisations – in Australia these include the Nine Network, the Fairfax organisation, News Ltd, the ABC – that receive the most visitors. Much of the content on these sites consists of repurposed materials extracted from their primary platform – headline stories or opinion columns from *The Australian*, for instance. The sites are structured in ways that carefully integrate the online material with the other media platforms in which the organisation has a commercial interest. So, *ninemsn* will allow us to watch video replays of episodes from *Sixty Minutes* or consult the *TV Guide*; the *Sydney Morning Herald* website will allow us to look through its photo galleries or its classifieds; and *ABC Online* will allow us to pull down transcripts of the latest edition of Radio National's *Media Report*. In most cases, these sites are simply a means of attracting consumers to a wider range of products than can be made visible within other media platforms. They do, however, offer a level of interactivity that constitutes a great increase over what is available through other platforms. The more populist the market addressed, by and large, the more interactivity. Most sites offer links to jobs, travel, lifestyle and consumer information, and the big US 24-hour-news sites such as *CNN* or *Fox News* offer the opportunity to select your own headline story from a large menu of running stories. Some like to run opinion polls on topics on the news: so visitors can record their vote on the performance of George Bush (Fox News), or the fate of Australian Guantanamo Bay prisoner David Hicks (*ninemsn*), and read what others have had to say on these topics. A more sophisticated and upmarket version of this is the web diary run by political commentator Margo Kingston on the *Sydney Morning Herald* site.

The current state of the political economy of the media, of course, means that the mainstream media outlets are not only in the best financial position to invest in this platform, but that they also have access to the largest and most varied reservoir of content to repurpose and place on their website. As we have seen already, there does seem to be a shift away from conventional media formats in terms of news and current affairs information, particularly for the younger demographic. However, this shift does not necessarily take these consumers out of the clutches of the major media organisations. Consuming one's news from the Nine network's *ninemsn* or the *Sydney Morning Herald's smh* may involve a change in consumer behaviour but it does not have much effect on the location of media power, or on the kinds of content available to the consumers of news in the marketplace. Despite the technological boosterism that can accompany predictions about the likely effects of what looks like an explosion of information sources, there is reason to be sceptical.

The Productivity Commission, probably inclined in that direction anyway, made precisely that point when it examined the need for revising media ownership regulations in 2000. As Fiona Martin interprets their conclusion, the commission argued that 'new online services, largely run by old media players, did not promise a significant increase in information diversity, and noted the trend towards repackaging of the same content for different purposes and outlets' (2004: 200). As a result, probably the greatest effect on the nature of the material available on the Internet comes from the contemporary dominance of online services by mainstream media organisations who think of the Internet as an ancillary platform and have so far resisted the need to think about how they might publish for the Internet as their first priority. This limits the capacity for online journalism to generate specific characteristics, let alone social or political effects, of its own. Online advertising revenues are starting to climb dramatically in Australia; indeed, online is now the fifth largest media sector for advertising expenditure. As this trend takes hold, it may become easier for media organisations which have their roots in earlier systems of delivery to see the Internet as the primary platform for certain kinds of media content. On the other hand, and running against the logic of an advertising-led development, it is probably *ABC Online* that has done the most, of the major media providers, to generate new, web-only, content and to open up access to users who want to contribute to news forums and the like.

Of course, and notwithstanding such a trend, we know very little yet about the extent to which we are likely to displace one kind of media consumption behaviour with another – routinely turning to the computer screen for one's news, for instance, rather than turning on the television. It is too early to tell if large numbers of consumers are likely to make that kind of adjustment as a more or less permanent shift in behaviour. The very existence of such a prospect, however, has already generated defensive developments within the older medium. The development of new capacities for digital television has focused upon delivering a much greater degree of interactivity, partly as a means of cutting out the potential competition from services delivered via the home computer. There are indications that broadcast television is already competing effectively with these new platforms by incorporating interactive aspects into their primetime programming, in particular by using SMS messaging as a means of enabling viewer interaction with the narrative on screen. In certain areas of broadcast television, there is a dramatic recovery of the large-scale national audience. What Jock Given refers to as the 'explosion of Event Television' – *The Block, Big Brother, Australian Idol*, the Rugby World Cup and so on – seems to him to be a 'counter-trend to the widely and accurately predicted fragmentation of a multi-channel and online universe': 'SMS, program websites, and other developments, strangely, seem to be boosting the social scale of these shared events, driving users back to the network screen... where advertisers are waiting for them.'[11] It is still too early to predict whether the much anticipated establishment of the home computer as the entertainment and information core of the post-modern household will actually eventuate; or whether it will continue to jockey around for a niche within a highly competitive technological home environment by offering access to those things that it does best. That is, it would not be offering movies, or sport, or drama programming in place of broadcast or pay TV, but it would be offering games, retail, banking, jobs, and connections to the full range of commercial and government information.

Midway between the established media sites and the grassroots/DIY/ amateur/activist alternative media sites is another group of news and current affairs sources on the Internet. This is exemplified in the Australian context by sites such as *crikey.com.au* or the more recent *Newmatilda.com.au*. These aim for the mainstream market but differentiate their approach from the mainstream providers by emphasising their independence, or their insistence on quality, or their traditional journalistic credentials. Importantly, it is typical of these sites that they address themselves not only to the alternative news audience but also to the current news producers – to journalists themselves. The pitch on the *crikey.com* home page makes this explicit:

> Are you sick of working for Big Kerry, Little Kerry, the Dirty Digger, young Lachlan, the shoe-string Canadians from Canwest, hair-brained magazines like *No Idea*, cash-strapped Aunty or even Fred Hilmer's Fairfax? Do you think the Australian media is too cautious, under-resourced, unadventurous and too concentrated? Then demonstrate a little bit of journalistic attitude and become a contributor to Australia's best known independent web site, www.crikey.com.au.

The site has a cheeky mode of self-presentation which might tend to recall the style (but perhaps not the content) of the *Drudge Report* :

> Crikey will point out theft, corruption, deception and collusion whenever and wherever it can. It is our self-appointed task to take a long thin spike to the bloated egos of political, media and corporate Australia and to take clear black and white snap shots of the men and women who have their fingers in the till or who simply get paid too much for doing shoddy work.

However, *Crikey* is genuinely focused upon providing an alternative outlet for news that other outlets will not print, and their commitment to this is evident in the fact that the site has been set up as much for frustrated journalists as for news audiences. They offer to print the story that 'the wimpy big media lawyers wouldn't clear'; they remind their contributors that they 'run anything on anyone without space constraints', and without the intervention of 'PR flaks'. Non-journalists, particularly whistleblowers, are made welcome but the core of the market to whom the site is pitched is clearly those who have been directly frustrated by current editorial practices within the mainstream media. For them, being on a site that picks up 70,000 page views per week is better than nothing at all – particularly when they can choose whether to contribute on or off the record.

In 2004, *crikey.com* had about 15 000 subscribers to its daily bulletins, 140 of them with parliamentary email addresses. The strength of the list of subscribers lies in who they are – politicians, journalists and other opinion makers – and Stephen Mayne, the site's founder, regards its influence on journalists as particularly important. Nonetheless, while he does see *crikey.com* as exerting some influence on media coverage and breaking 'little stories that the rest of the media can make a bigger thing about', he was quick to hose down exaggerated claims for the influence of online journalism on the 2004 election: 'the internet won't have a fundamental effect on this election campaign. It might be 3 or 4 per cent compared with old media' (cited in MacLean, 2004b: 17).

A more sedate version of this kind of website is *Newmatilda.com*, set up in August 2004 by John Menadue (a former head of the Prime Minister's Department) on the coat-tails of the 'truth in government' open

letter addressed to the Howard government by the 43 ex-public servants –
or as National Party MP De-Anne Kelly called them at the time, the 'dod-
dering daiquiri diplomats'. *New Matilda* is an online magazine, structured
along the traditional lines of the weekly news and comment magazine and
adapted to the Internet platform. Like *crikey.com* it also foregrounds its
independent journalistic mission. According to its home page, *New
Matilda* is committed to 'truth in public life, independent political commentary, policy based in public good, and citizen power in decision making'
– a traditional liberal set of principles and one for which there is no
shortage of willing writers and commentators. Contributors to the first
issue included well known political journalists Christine Wallace, Greg
Barns and Margo Kingston. In addition, the use of pseudonyms indicates
that, like *crikey.com*, *New Matilda* will act as an outlet for moonlighting
journalists unwilling to go on the record, as well as for the occasional
whistleblower. Their sports report, curiously enough, is produced under
the pseudonym of 'Trackie Dax', with the note that the writer is a 'doctor
who loves sport' – inviting us to guess who it actually is. In an interview
with the *Media* section of *The Australian* to announce the web magazine's
launch, Menadue described the venture as a response to 'probably the
greatest institutional failure of our age'; he says, 'with a few notable exceptions, under-resourced journalists are no match for political and corporate
media managers'. 'Unable to compete on hard news and analysis, the
media has increasingly turned to infotainment, opinion, gossip and snug-
gling up to power.' As result, Menadue says he acted on some advice his
father had once given him: 'Stop complaining and do something about it'
(cited in MacLean, 2004a: 43).

Those behind *New Matilda* may not like being lumped together with a
brash and noisy upstart like *crikey.com* (in MacLean's piece in *The
Australian*, *New Matilda* editor Natasha Cica bridled at such a suggestion,
saying their site serves 'an entirely different purpose'), and they certainly
adopt very different styles in the way they present their content.
Nevertheless, they do operate in similar territory. In fact, it is notable that
virtually all of the non-mainstream versions of online journalism we have
been examining in this chapter share a common set of defining positions:
they enjoy their principled independence from the major media organisations, they are critical of the current establishment (if not of the
Establishment, per se), and they are utterly convinced of the failure of the

conventional media to provide a proper public service. They offer their stories both as a goad to the mass media, and as an alternative source of information. In terms of how they present their material (and here *New Matilda* is an exception), there are unexpected similarities between their mission and that of what I might call the Michael Moore version of contemporary current affairs that we examined in chapter 4: the interesting way in which a more entertainment-oriented, even tabloid, style of presentation has collaborated with a liberal-cum-activist commitment to developing a better informed public. Like the developments I discussed in chapter 4, many examples of what I have called online journalism are in fact keen to explicitly differentiate what they do from journalism. In relation to the alternative news networks such as Indymedia, the label of 'post-journalism' is probably quite apposite.

On the other hand, and just as we found at the end of chapter 4 when I reported the recent growth in the audiences for US public radio news services, there are other instances which are clearly committed to reinvigorating the traditional ideals and practices of independent journalism. In such sites, journalism remains the goal, and current practice is the problem. *New Matilda* would be unlikely to identify their project as an activist one, and theirs is the most conventional of the sites I have discussed in terms of the journalistic mission it serves. Nonetheless, like all of the sites mentioned, it too is motivated by a sense that the media no longer serves the public, and by the need for a more committed, less spuriously objective, and more fearless form of journalism to counteract the quiescence of their more cynical, anodyne and commercial counterparts. Crucially, and there is something of a sting in this tail, it is important to recognise that it is comparatively easy for online journalism to take that kind of idealistic position. The costs of publishing on the web are so much less than any other form of publishing that it is little wonder that it can operate with less regard to such limitations. Furthermore, there are ethical regimes which may not seem to easily encompass the Internet journalism sites but which other platforms such as free-to-air television ignore at their peril (nonetheless, even Crikey has had its fingers burnt from time to time as well). So, in some important respects, it is not a level playing field; online journalism benefits from its modest cost structure, from the fact that many are prepared to publish on the web for a fraction of the fees they would expect from the print media, and from that the fact that it does not have to provide the kind of comprehensive news service carried by the major metropolitan news papers or electronic outlets. The activist model suits the political economy of, and industrial structure for, the online sites very well and so it is hardly surprising, on the one hand, that this kind of model has proliferated and, on the other, that the dominant model to which they offer an alternative is that provided by organisations who have already funded their news service through another platform of delivery.

My research into this sector does not support the view that it now constitutes a convincing alternative to broadcast and pay TV, radio or the press. It is still the case that only a small minority seek their news and current affairs diet primarily from the Internet – even though that minority is certainly growing.[12] If we are to go by the hit-rate on the various news sites, then the political economy of the news industry remains largely unchanged by the developments we have been examining in this part of the chapter. However, one does not have to look for long among the competing news sites on the Internet to find that, bubbling beneath this overarching trend, there is a strong sense of dissatisfaction with other media formats and a conviction of the need for a more independent, public-good-oriented and committed news media. Accompanying this is a demand for greater interactivity and participation, particularly from younger audiences, which suggests that they are concerned by their restricted access to the mechanisms which produce news as well as by the restricted range of content they find in mainstream news formats. That means that it is not improbable to look to online journalism as a growing source of news, but also as a competing model for the production of news – particularly political news. Addressing consumers as news producers, as collaborators, does seem to be a novel and probably significant shift in the way news production has thought of itself, and that is the way in which online journalism may exercise its most important influence in the future. Now, however, there is simply not enough traction, not enough independent sources, and not enough influence on the mainstream news agenda, to argue that it constitutes a sufficient alternative to the services provided by television, radio or the press.

For some, of course, this is not the case. Certainly it would appear that among the younger audience in particular, those who find satisfying alternatives in the Internet news sites are also those who are most alienated from mainstream television current affairs. If that is the case, we may be watching the incubation of the news production and consumption cultures of the future as these sites proliferate and develop into a mature sector of the media industry. However, I don't think we should have to wait on that eventuality. The situation I have been describing throughout this book is not one that Australians should accept as a permanent condition of their media environment. In the final chapter, I want to outline some basic reasons why I hold that view – why the current performance of Australian television current affairs matters.

NOTES

1   This first section is a revised version of my article 'First Contact: Coming to Terms with the Cable Guy', *UTS Review*, 3:2, November, 1997.

2   The main instances include Moran (1985), Moran & O'Regan (1989), Tulloch & Turner (1989), Cunningham & Miller (1994), Cunningham & Jacka (1996), Given (1998), Turner & Cunningham (2000), McKee (2001), and the relevant sections of Cunningham & Turner (2002).

3   Wark says:

> The massive presence in the media flow of American stories, images, faces, voices, is sometimes all that stabilises the flow of meanings in the global media net. Take away America's imaginary domination and the domination of the imaginary by America, and meaning would drift and eddy, caught in an impossible turbulence and glide. (1994: 14)

4   A term used in cultural studies to describe the way we can be invited to be part of a discourse, almost irresistibly, by the way it is framed. Here, it means the way in which the presenter assumes we are with them, and in turn that we will allow them to speak on our behalf.

5   The title of his 1994 book.

6   Literary theorist Hans Robert Jauss, in *Aesthetic Experience and Literary Hermeneutics*, (1982), classified modalities of reception which influenced the process of '[i]dentification with the character in the literary text': his system included associative identification, admiring identification, sympathetic identification, cathartic identification, and ironic modality. David Marshall's *Celebrity and Power: Fame in Contemporary Culture* usefully appropriates Jauss' system to explain, among other things, television's privileging of the sympathetic mode of identification: where 'there is solidarity with the character or suffering personality. We place ourselves in the position of the hero' (1997: 68–71).

7   Brand & Pearson, *Sources of News*, ABA 2001. Available on the ABA website, <http://www.aba.gov.au/tv/research/projects/sources>.

9   This is how their website describes its mission:

> ElectionTracker.net is targeted at Australians under 30 who want to get some straightforward info to help them make an informed decision on who they'll vote for on Saturday, 9 October (and those interested in what Australians under 30 think about the election issues). You'll find loads of background info on the different political parties and their policies, a

wide variety of perspectives on key election issues as they relate to young people, and a whole bunch of other cool & interesting election-related stuff. One of the most exciting aspects of the electionTracker.net project is that four young 'electionTrackers' will be travelling on the campaign trail itself, following either John Howard or Mark Latham around for a week, delivering important insights into the election by writing daily articles and blogging their personal experiences. These talented young reporters, selected from a nation-wide call for applications, will deliver unique youth perspectives from the heart of the campaign trail, keeping close eye on all policy announcements that affect young people. ElectionTracker.net also features discussion forums and allows readers to have their say on the news, interviews and analysis that appear on the website. All ElectionTracker content is generated by talented young writers from all over Australia. The website also takes a humorous look at all things election-related, on its ElectionSlacker section – a source of satire, silliness and all sorts of light-heartedness. Accessed 30/9/2004.

10 See the discussion of the digital commons by Rennie and Young in Goggin, 2004 (242–257).

11 Jock Given's contribution to the 'Histories, trends, futures' online forum convened by Gerard Goggin and Geert Lovink, and published in Goggin, 2004 (283).

12 A recent, so far unpublished, study by An Nguyen, titled 'The power of online news: myth or reality?', emerging from his PhD research at the University of Queensland, found that 29 per cent of those who responded to his survey said that they used online news sources – but only 36 per cent of these turned to the Internet as their first-choice news medium.

CHAPTER SEVEN

Why does current affairs television matter?

The public conversation

In chapter 2, I described how, when *This Day Tonight* ceased production in 1978, its demise seemed to reflect the weight of industry opinion which doubted that current affairs formats could any longer attract a mass audience. The Nine Network flagship, *A Current Affair*, was also taken off air in 1978, despite Kerry Packer regarding it as providing him with the 'political muscle' he needed to make politicians pay attention (Stone,2000: 162). It looked as if the well of political current affairs had run dry. As we saw earlier, some suggested that the audience's enthusiasm for current affairs programming through the late 1960s and early 1970s may have been a consequence of the volatile political mood in the nation at that time – the mood which saw Whitlam triumphantly elected and then controversially dismissed within three years – rather than of any long-term loyalty to the format. As things quietened down politically, the orthodoxy holds, maybe the audience was ready to turn to other formats and other interests. Despite the centrality of news and information to the charter of the ABC, as well as to the licenses of the commercial free-to-air proprietors, it is perhaps not surprising that many thought the trend had worked itself out and a strategic withdrawal was required. On the Nine Network, this involved turning over the *ACA* timeslot to the popular soap opera, *The Sullivans*, while it considered its next move.

It is remarkable how effective that next move proved to be. In 1979, *Sixty Minutes* rolled into town as the 'current affairs spectacular'[1] with a $2 million per annum budget and a gaggle of star reporters. It had a worrying slow start with single-digit ratings in the first week, but its word-of-mouth was strong. According to its founding producer, Gerald Stone, there is a myth that it took the program two years to become viable when in fact, he claims, it only took five weeks to rate in the 'promising teens'; from then on, Stone says, it climbed steadily until it was clearly a major hit (2000: 184). *Sixty Minutes* went on to handsomely repay the network's investment as it became Australia's most successful current affairs program ever. It is worth reminding ourselves that it did this by providing a blend of strong investigative stories such as Ray Martin's Appin mine reports and dramatic political interviews such as George Negus's legendary confrontation with Margaret Thatcher on the one hand, and shameless celebrity flirt-pieces (Mike Munro interviewing Dolly Parton springs to mind here) and high-profile cheque-book exclusives with persons in the news (Lindy Chamberlain, the 'iceman' James Scott, and so on) on the other. For the most part, its stars presented themselves as journalists first and foremost, with George Negus in exotic locations wearing his blue jeans and R.M.Williams boots generating an iconic image of the adventurous Aussie reporter.

Once the *Sixty Minutes* juggernaut had shown the way, current affairs gradually revived to the point where it became *the* hot format. As I have noted earlier in this book, the mid-1980s to the mid-1990s was the boom period for launching new current affairs programs. Significantly, this happened across both the commercial and the public sector and all over the schedule; current affairs was not confined to the traditional 6.30–7.30 pm timeslot but popped up in other prime-time slots as well. In 1988 alone, four new programs started: these were the Ten Network's *Face to Face* with Kerry O'Brien and the big budget one-hour *Page One*; the Seven Network's *Hinch*; and the ABC's *Sunday Conference* with Michael Shildberger. This was in addition to continuing programs from the ABC (*The 7.30 Report*), the Nine Network (the revived *A Current Affair*, *Sixty Minutes*), and SBS (*Dateline*). At its peak, the current affairs boom had 15 programs on air between 1992 and 1994 which ranged from the high quality *Foreign Correspondent* (ABC) to the tabloid *Hard Copy* and *Alan Jones Live* (both Ten).[2] While the tabloid shows certainly were key contributors to the boom, it is also worth remembering that *A Current Affair* had Jana Wendt operating at her peak as a political interviewer during this period. Indeed, one contemporary report described her performance as 'part queen, part cobra' in what became a celebrated interview with Sir Joh Bjelke Petersen (Button, 1990: 6), in which he was reduced to threatening her, on air, with retribution. Far from swamping the market with this much product, the Australian Broadcasting Tribunal's annual review of broadcasting for 1992 found that news and current affairs programs were among the most popular, with *A Current Affair* and *Sixty Minutes* scoring higher than the leading comedies and local drama series (Moodie and Della-Giacoma, 1992: 5).

At the same time, however, we can detect a rising groundswell of analysis and criticism of the performance of these programs, and in particular of changes in their performance over time. In a special feature for *Saturday Extra*'s 'News Wars' supplement in *The Age* in 1990, Peter Wilmoth and James Button laid out what are now the familiar criticisms: that the news and current affairs agenda was driven by ratings and privileged those stories with strong visuals; that audiences were attracted by the heavily promoted personas of the program presenters; and that the standard mode of reporting was too sensationalist (1990: 1, 6). In short, it was what I described in chapter 3 as the whole tabloidisation agenda. A 'softer' version of current affairs was tried, and actually seemed to work when Seven's *Real Life* took on *A Current Affair* in 1993, apparently appealing more successfully to a female audience and encouraging Nine to draft Ray Martin from *The Midday Show*. It didn't last long, however. By 1995, we start to hear the early articulations of what has since become something of a mantra – that this year's crop of current affairs programs would return to 'hard' news, to serious topics, and discontinue the 'soft' lifestyle stories. The successor to *Real Life* was *Today Tonight* and it was promoted by Seven's Director of News and Current Affairs, Terry Plane, in 1995 as a return to the core mission of current affairs: '*Today Tonight* will be more topical, traditional, straightforward and not afraid to ask the hard questions', he said (Freeman, 1995: 1,6).

We have been hearing renditions of that same old song from every television current affairs program ever since, but little has changed. The story I have been telling through this book is partly about how difficult it appears to be for commercial current affairs programs to return to their core business – not necessarily because they don't think it is worthwhile but because their reading of their market keeps on challenging their nerve. Ironically, at the same time as their reading of the market is used to justify the inclusion of more entertainment-oriented stories, public criticism of television current affairs has increasingly focused on its cynicism, its triviality, and its distortion of journalism's original mission. A cover story in the *Bulletin* in 1996 was headlined 'Why People Hate The Media' and it reported the results of a survey of public attitudes to news and current affairs, journalists and commentators, and the reliability of the media. According to this *Bulletin* survey, 85 per cent of respondents thought that there was too much emphasis on sex and violence, 80 per cent thought that the media did not care about people's feelings and their right to privacy and only 16 per cent responded positively to the proposition that journalists behaved in a trustworthy manner in the way they obtain and present stories (Murphy, 1996: 14–17). This was only one early instance of the many reports that emerged from the mid-1990s onwards to question the kind of service Australians were receiving from these programs as the process of hybridisation – from news and information to entertainment formats – gradually progressed.[3]

As I argued in chapter 1, and as we have seen throughout this book, there is every reason for such criticism to be aired. While the hybrid formats have doggedly pursued their ever more elusive down-market audience, the pursuit of the traditional objectives of current affairs journalism has been increasingly sporadic. Whole areas of public affairs have been ignored while we have learnt about how effective the latest low-carb diet has been for Janine and Damien from Balgowlah who are trying to shed ten kilos each in the two months left before they are due to marry in swimsuits at the water's edge on Bondi Beach. The cultural, social and political role that this format can – *should* – perform for Australian citizens has been progressively abrogated in order to do what most of the other formats do already – that is, to just entertain. Of course, we may well have been entertained from time to time, but this format has the capacity to do so much more. Think of some of the moments when it has lived up to its potential. These days such moments seem only to occur at points of high crisis, when news and current affairs programs are jolted into remembering the importance of their core function. Most recently, I was impressed with Michael Usher's graphic reports for *National Nine News* and *A Current Affair* from the Beslan school massacre in southern Russia in 2004, but there are many other memorable moments in the recent past: Ten's Sandra Sully's marathon stint attempting to make sense of September 11 overnight, for instance, and Sarah Henderson's extraordinary 7.30 Report interview with 'Lynne', the nurse who witnessed the Port Arthur massacre, which won a Walkley for the ABC. At such moments, the value of this form of programming is palpable. Unfortunately, however, it seems as if it is only at such historic points that even those working in current affairs are able to fully believe in its importance. That they exploit its potential so rarely constitutes more than a decade of lost opportunity.

What is particularly frustrating is that the opportunity we still have before us is fast receding in other national and regional markets around the world. Unlike, for instance, the North American market, the Australian television market is still dominated by free-to-air broadcasting and even with its current content preferences it is still possible for news and current affairs programs to generate a national, public, conversation about what are regarded as the important issues of the day. That the media should provide the conditions for such a conversation to take place seems fundamental to me. That is not just an old-fashioned, academic, industry outsider's view. Explicit – even now – in the current regulatory regimes for broadcasters are formal statements about the fundamental importance of news, information and informed debate to the media's contribution to a democratic society. These statements still reflect a conception of broadcasting – including commercial broadcasting – that regards it as a national service; they embody a principled resistance to the idea that it is enough for broadcasters to address the market rather than the citizenry. Of course, it is in the areas of news and information where these considerations are clearly paramount and where the community rightly expects to receive a dividend for licensing the media proprietors to operate a scarce and restricted national resource – a spot on the broadcasting spectrum. That dividend is currently being withheld in favour of what are, misguidedly in my view, seen as the pre-eminent commercial considerations. In this context, then, as citizens we need to insist that the regulatory authorities should enforce the principle that current affairs programming remains a fundamentally important means of creating a public sphere where debate may occur. What happens to this form of programming is of more than commercial concern.

You have to ask, though, how many in the media still seem to care about such principles. A related issue which emerged in public debate during the mid-1990s, and which has been a continuing thread throughout much of my discussion in this book, involves the power of current affairs programs: the degree of responsibility with which that power has been exercised, the extent to which it can be limited, and the processes of redress made available to its victims. This was especially vigorously debated in 1993 when *A Current Affair*'s Mike Munro allegedly broke a police air-exclusion zone during a siege at Cangai near Grafton, creating operational difficulties for police at the scene where two children were being held hostage by a suspected killer, Leonard Leabeter. Most extraordinarily, *ACA*'s host, Mike Willesee spoke by telephone directly with Leabeter and with one of the children on-air; during the latter conversation he deliberately invited the child to consider whether they were in any danger. This was widely regarded as having jeopardised the operation's objective of bringing the siege to a safe conclusion and was angrily criticised by the police involved. So well known was this incident, and the ethical concerns it raised, that it turned up in a slightly fictionalised version as the basis for an episode of the ABC comedy-satire *Frontline* in 1994 (see Williams, 1994: 12).

As we saw in chapter 4, the irresponsibile performance of current affairs journalism has been an issue for at least a decade. It is, though, a specific instance within a much broader concern about how much power is now available to the media organisations, and how powerless the rest of us are to counter it. Not only are the remaining media complaints procedures more or less worthless, but the media remain reluctant to surrender any of their authority by admitting and correcting mistakes or even by behaving in a conciliatory manner when disputes arise. To underline the comprehensiveness and remorselessness of the power of the media in action, it is worth listening to some of those who have been subject to it.

In *Media Tarts*, her account of how the Australian press represents female politicians, Julia Baird examines the way the careers of particular women in politics – Cheryl Kernot, Pauline Hanson, and Carmen Lawrence among them – have been shaped or influenced by the nature of their treatment in the media. I should stress that this is a long way from a predictable 'the boys in the media set out to get her' story; Baird provides quite nuanced accounts of the varied roles the media played in particular instances. What is never in doubt, though, is the amount of power available – the media's capacity to literally make or break a politician – as well as the relatively unpredictable manner in which that power is exercised. Baird cites comments of Democrat Senator Natasha Stott-Despoja, revealing her astonishment at how much power the Canberra press gallery has at its disposal:

> The level of influence the media has [is] totally extraordinary, just amazing, and certainly was beyond my wildest dreams. I will never underestimate the role of the media in Australian political life... I think the media is actually culpable in selecting, electing, producing leaders and determining who stays. (Baird, 2004: 162)

The account presented in Baird's book raises serious doubts about how rationally and responsibly this influence is exercised. Time and again, she documents how the media behave as a pack – turning on victims because they are vulnerable, without much thought to what might be the end in view. She cites ABC journalist Monica Attard's reflections about the media's treatment of former Democrat leader and high-profile convert to the ALP, Cheryl Kernot:

> I suddenly got a taste of how intense the media scrutiny was of her and how difficult it was, not being able to walk around your suburb, in which you lived, not being able to leave your apartment or answer your phone. I could see it in her face ... What did we want? Did we want Cheryl to top herself? ... It's the ugly side of the Australian media when we pick, pick, hound, hound, hound, and what do we want from that person? (Baird, 2004: 270)

It is a chilling insight: that there simply is no brake on the process, as this extraordinary power is in the hands of those who exercise it because they can, not because they have a specific objective in mind. There is no means through which the media can collectively say, 'enough'. Instead, the pressure will only cease when they move on to a better story.

These are commercial, competitive pressures, of course, but it is also true that news journalism is like that; it has short-term professional objectives and can't afford to stand back and reflect for too long because events will have moved on. News journalism provides us with access to action and events more easily than to analysis or understanding. The latter task is best performed by current affairs journalism, and it is a task that must be performed. To have news without analysis is simply dangerous; we have a glimpse of that these days in the incoherence of the reporting of Islamic fundamentalism, where almost nobody knows anything which can explain it to us. And yet, this is the situation we are approaching as current affairs journalism grinds itself into oblivion by repeating the same tired formats, doing what it thinks it must to seek the killer rating, and turning journalism into just another genre of entertainment.

So, why does television current affairs matter?

There are many ways of addressing this question, as television current affairs programming has the capacity to play significant political, social, and cultural roles in Australian society. I believe that there remains a core public function for current affairs, one that we all recognise even if we choose not to watch programs which perform it. The value of an independent, reliable and ethical means of interrogating the news of the day, while providing informed and expert comment, is fundamental to an open democratic society. The regulatory structures for broadcasting in Australia clearly regard the provision of news and information as a fundamental requirement for licensees and it is explicitly written into the charters of the SBS and the ABC.

The issue raised by the story I have been telling over the last six chapters is this. I think it is the case that current affairs programming did once play a useful and effective role by scrutinising and analysing the behaviour of government, private institutions, business and society at large. If that role is no longer being played by the current crop of formats, and if there has been no alternative format developed which might effectively take over that role, then we need to ask if something important to our society is in danger of being lost. My answer to that question is 'yes'. If there is no longer any equivalent of the service current affairs once provided, then we have a net reduction in the range of the basic democratic furniture our society has provided for us.

This raises quite fundamental questions about the role of the media in today's society – a society which has surrendered so much to the market, to user-pays, and to the commercialisation of all kinds of practices that were once run according to quite different principles. Somewhere along the line, these earlier, quite different, principles simply drop out of the picture and lose their cultural purchase. An example of what I mean can be drawn from the upheavals caused in the BBC over the David Kelly affair in 2003–4. The decision of reporter Andrew Gilligan to 'sex up' his weapons of mass destruction story had enormous repercussions: tragically claiming the life of Gilligan's informant, Kelly, as well as, later, the job of the BBC's otherwise highly successful Managing Director, Greg Dyke. The BBC commissioned an internal review of its practices as a result of this controversy and the report it produced argued that the organisation needed to restate and re-affirm its 'core values'.[4] The report suggested that a raft of small but incremental shifts in the BBC's practice, occurring over many years and widely dispersed through the organisation, had actually changed the nature of what they did. Among the news and current affairs practices nominated as participating in such a process were the use of 'single source' stories, the use of the live 'two-way', and the failure to provide, as a matter of fairness, formal opportunities for people to respond on-air to serious claims made against them. These practices are all rife in contemporary current affairs programming in Australia as well. Further, the BBC report restated the principle of accountability – the importance of the BBC admitting their mistakes, apologising and learning from them. This has never been a comfortable part of the news culture in Australia, and it is certainly not part of the production culture in television current affairs. I referred earlier to the macho ethic ruling this culture, drawing on Ellen Fanning's SBS series, A Fine Line; as we saw then, it is not a culture that willingly admits mistakes.

Finally, the social and political value of the news media was re-affirmed in the BBC report through reference to the importance of their 'striving to be an independent monitor of powerful individuals and bodies, making judgments on an editorial rather than a commercial basis', and 'prioritising stories of significance to audiences'. Again, it is precisely this kind of independent, fourth-estate, role that has gone missing in recent years in Australia.

As a country, I want to insist, Australia is very much the poorer for such failings – for these shifts in both principle and practice. Over the last few years there has been a number of major political debates where the majority or government line has been almost automatically reflected in the media's treatment of the issues concerned. The examples I have in mind include the children overboard/Tampa issue in 2001, and the Australian military commitment to the so-called 'coalition of the willing' in Iraq in 2003 – but there could be many more. In both these instances, criticism of the government position was dismissed as un-Australian, naïve, and was really not seriously considered in much of the media (the significant exception on the children overboard matter was *The Australian* newspaper, and on Iraq, the ABC). Indeed, those who dared to express contrary opinions were subjected, at times, to something close to vilification. We now know that on both of these issues the government position was deeply flawed – by a cynical manipulation of fear and racism in the case of the refugees and by poor assessments of intelligence information motivated by a desire to accommodate the United States in the commitment to the war on Iraq. Closing down debate on these, both genuinely contentious, issues has proved to be an illiberal and ill-informed move that unnecessarily acceded to the dominant politics of the moment. It is pre-eminently the job of the media to treat government explanations with scepticism in order to test rigorously the legitimacy and public benefit of their decisions – and we need this to occur at the time, not years later. For the most part, in relation to these two issues, the Australian media cynically followed what they perceived to be the popular mood of the time – a xenophobic and utterly irrational fear of being 'swamped' by refugees, and (less popular but probably still marginally the majority view) the conviction that there was a relation between the attack on Iraq and the war on terror. Even when those sections of the media that did not take the populist option raised questions about these positions, the rest of the media was clearly disinclined to follow suit.

It is hard to know, categorically, how and why this situation has come about – although it does recall some of the issues addressed in the discussion of television current affairs and the treatment of politics in chapter 2. One likely possibility is that the current situation reflects the comprehensive reorientation of the media around its commercial function. We are living at a time when the notion that the media should be aggressively independent in their pursuit of accurate information, in the first place, and politically accountable to the citizenry, in the second place, has largely been displaced by the convenient notion that the media are, first and foremost, commercial businesses whose primary responsibility is to their shareholders. Ours is a media formation which most easily identifies with the interests of business and of government – rather than with those of the public. *That* kind of media we simply don't need – but by and large that is what we have. Furthermore, there is every sign that the increasing professional isolation of those who work in the media is encouraging a workplace culture which believes ultimately in its own expertise and is not interested in that of its audiences. The fetish of the insider's knowledge, an occupational hazard in journalism that takes on its most bullying incarnation in television, reinforces the complacency and irresponsibility that enables this situation to continue.

The ideological conversion to seeing their role as primarily a commercial one has been a gradual and often uncomfortable process for many Australian journalists but as this now matures into something approaching an orthodoxy (and not an unchallenged one, I admit) we can see the effects it engenders. The gradual disappearance of current affairs from commercial radio is one instance, and there is a distinct danger that this could be followed by the disappearance of current affairs from television. The logic of the history I have been outlining, for instance, is for the industry to keep flogging the dead horse of its weary old formats until they lose their audience entirely. At that point, the networks can claim to have proved there is no market for current affairs programs any more, and replace them with a game show. And yet, as recent events have so clearly demonstrated, the Australian community needs the benefit of *more* independent scrutiny – in particular of public policy, institutional politics, and corporate ethics – not less.

There is another dimension to be considered here. Simon Cottle, Professor of Media and Communication at the University of Melbourne, has written about the important role that journalism plays in constructing our relationship with the rest of the culture. The forms of journalism, he says, 'mediate surrounding conflicts and contending interests and, depending on how they do this, so they serve variously to either enhance or undermine the "public sphere(s)" of engaged citizenship'. Journalism does more than just provide access to information. In their facilitation of an engaged cultural citizenship, journalists must interpret and negotiate 'social conflicts, the play of discursive positions and the struggle by different interests for cultural recognition and public legitimacy' (Cottle, 2001: 61). A complex role for the journalist, obviously, and one that I don't want to underestimate or minimise. Cultural citizenship includes rights not only to information but also the access to a full range of social experiences, to knowledge that is not confined to one or two 'frameworks of interpretation', and to personal participation in the activities of the society.[5] As Cottle goes on to say, television journalism is probably the 'citizenship genre *par excellence*', as it 'delegates access and conditions public participation and the representation of contending views and experiences' (62). What arguments such as these emphasise is the special cultural significance of this television genre in producing the conditions within which citizens can most freely and productively participate in a democracy.

This is not some 'chattering classes', 'cultural elite', issue; rather, it reminds us of how fundamental the media are to the ways in which citizenship in the contemporary nation-state is constructed and performed. Simply, the way we learn about our society, the way we participate in its decisions and debates, the way we construct our personal and community identities, and the stories we tell ourselves to explain the particular nature of our culture and society, are all framed, negotiated and developed in some way through the media. The argument I have been making throughout this book is that television news and current affairs have been among the most important components of this process. Consequently, the quality of their performance – the manner in which programs actually do, or do not, 'enhance or undermine the public sphere' – matters a great deal. What I have been trying to do in this book is to focus upon just that – the quality of their performance today and its consequences.

Another thing I have tried to do here is to provide a little perspective, a longer view of the history of current affairs in Australia. What happens when you take this slightly longer historical perspective is that you see how easily, and how dramatically, trends such as the one we are currently experiencing can be turned around. *This Day Tonight* came out the blue to be a major ratings success, inventing a whole new genre for Australian television, and operating as a much-valued institution for the majority of its 11 years on air. *Sixty Minutes* arrived at a time when television current affairs seemed least commercially viable and wound up serving the Australian public, for better and for worse, for the next 25 years – and it is still going strong. Both of these were new ideas which broke with the industry wisdom prevailing at the time and pioneered new formats that took the news and current affairs mission seriously – no matter how differently that translated into the kind of programs they became. The time is now ripe for another adventurous television programmer to grasp the opportunity – an opportunity that may be receding as we speak – to find a means of reviving the original mission of television current affairs into a viable format again. Maybe some of the histories outlined in this book might indicate how that might be done.

That is the aspirational message of the book; the more realistic one is a little less hopeful. At the moment, much of what passes for current affairs on Australian television does not particularly matter. Worse, continuing not to matter, and perhaps even mattering progressively less, threatens to run down the format and devalue the currency of current affairs programming over time. To repair that situation will require a major reinvestment in the format and in the possibility that it could actually exert, in Packer's words, some 'political muscle'. The contemporary version of current affairs now occasionally pretends that it is interested in having an effect, but we all know that really most of it isn't. Returning to that kind of agenda is going to involve critically dealing with major social and political and cultural issues again, as well as the domestic and the personal. In my view, unless television current affairs is prepared to take that route, then not only is there not much of a future for it, but it won't matter to most of us whether it has a future or not. We'll be stuck with having to invent another means of generating a public conversation about the things that do matter.

NOTES

1   Sandra Hall's *Bulletin* article (1979: 54–60) was headed, 'Television: Now it's the Current Affairs Spectacular'.
2   The source for these details is Harrison's *The Australian Film and Television Companion* (1994).
3   As I write, yet another survey of this kind has been published, this time by Eric Beecher of *The Reader* magazine (see MacLean, 2004: 18).
4   BBC News: At-a-glance: BBC post-Hutton Report, <http://news.bbc.co.uk/go/pr/fr/-2/hi/entertainment/3831831.stm> Accessed 15/7/ 2004.
5   See Cottle, 2001, where he draws upon Graham Murdock's formulation of this idea (61–62).

References

Altheide, D & Snow, R (1991) *Media Worlds in the Postjournalism Era*, Aldine de Gruyter, New York.

Anderson, D (1992) 'Waiting for Robbo', *Sydney Morning Herald, Guide*, 25–31 May: 6.

Baird, J (2004) *Media Tarts: How the Australian Press Frames Female Politicians*, Scribe, Melbourne.

Bell, P (1998) 'ABC News, 7.30 *Report* and "Waterfront Dispute(s)"', <http://www.abc.net.au/corp/pubs.bell1.pdf>

Bonner, F (2003a) *Ordinary Television*, Sage, London.

—— (2003b) 'Testimonial current affairs: The *Australian Story* approach to celebrity', unpublished paper presented to 'New(s) Times' conference, University of Melbourne, December.

Brand, J & Pearson, M (2001) *Sources of News*, Australian Broadcasting Authority, Sydney, <http://www.aba.gov.au/tv/research/projects/sources>.

Bromley, M (2001) (ed.) *No News is Bad News: Radio, Television and the Public*, Longmans, Harlow.

Bruns, A (2004) 'Reconfiguring journalism: syndication, gatewatching and multiperspectival news' in G.Goggin (ed.) *Virtual Nation: The Internet in Australia*, UNSW Press, Sydney: 77–192.

Button, J (1990) 'Racing to number 1 in current affairs', *Age*, 28 April, 'News Wars' supplement: 6.

Casimir, J (1998) 'The big turn-off', *Sydney Morning Herald, Guide*, 22–28 June: 4–5.

Clark, P (1998) 'Crudities and condoms: Alston's racy ABC letters', *Sydney Morning Herald*, 20 July: 5.

Cottle, S (2001) 'Television news and citizenship: packaging the public sphere' in

M.Bromley (ed.) *No News is Bad News: Radio, Television and the Public,* Longmans, Harlow: 61–79.

Couch, S (1994) 'New attitude', *Sydney Morning Herald, Guide,* 8 August: 5.

Couldry, N (2003) *Media Rituals: A Critical Approach,* Routledge, London and New York.

Crouch, W (1972a) 'The ABC of TDT', *Bulletin,* 2 September: 19–21.

—— (1972b) 'TDT – But by any other name?', *Bulletin,* 14 October: 25.

Cunningham, S & Jacka, E (1996) *Australian Television and International Mediascapes,* Cambridge University Press, Cambridge.

Cunningham, S & Miller, T (1994) (eds) *Contemporary Australian Television,* UNSW Press, Sydney.

Cunningham, S & Turner, G (2002) (eds) *The Media and Communications in Australia,* Allen & Unwin, Sydney.

Day, M (2004) 'Aunty takes a reality check', *Australian,* September 18–19: 21.

Ellis, J (1982) *Visible Fictions: Cinema, Television, Video,* Routledge and Kegan Paul, London.

Evans, V & Sternberg, J (2000) 'Young people, politics and television current affairs in Australia', *Journal of Australian Studies,* 63: 103–109.

Fanning, E (2004) 'Telling tales reveal home truths', *Australian, Media,* 22 April: 16.

Figeon, R & Ellis S (1998) 'Ratings slumps have hit current affairs', *Herald-Sun, Guide,* 17 June: 10–11.

Flew, T (2002) *New Media: An Introduction,* Oxford University Press, Melbourne.

Franklin, B (1998) *Newszak and News Media,* Edward Arnold, London.

Freeman, J (1995) 'Hard news: will current affairs grow teeth in '95?', *Sydney Morning Herald, Guide,* 23–29 January: 1, 6.

Gibbons, P (1971) 'Shipp and TDT: a reply', *Quadrant,* September/October: 90–96.

Gill, R (1993) 'Beware the Brat Pack', *Age, Green Guide,* 11 March: 2.

Gitlin, T (1997) 'The anti-populism of cultural studies', in M Ferguson & P Golding (eds) *Cultural Studies in Question,* Sage, London: 25–38.

Given, J (1998) *The Death of Broadcasting? Media's Digital Future,* UNSW Press, Sydney.

—— (2003) *Turning off the Television: Broadcasting's Uncertain Future,* UNSW Press, Sydney.

Glover, R (1988) 'Robbo's war', *Sydney Morning Herald, Good Weekend,* 25–26 October: 12.

Goggin, G (2004) (ed.) *Virtual Nation: The Internet in Australia,* UNSW Press, Sydney.

Goggin, G & Lovink, G (2004) 'Histories, trends, futures: a round table on the Australian internet', in G.Goggin (ed.) *Virtual Nation: The Internet in Australia,* UNSW Press, Sydney: 274–291.

Hall, Sandra (1979) 'Television: now it's the current affairs spectacular', *Bulletin,* 13 February: 54–60.

Hall, Stuart (1982) 'The rediscovery of "ideology": the return of the repressed in media studies' in M.Gurevitch, T.Bennett, J.Curran, & J. Woollacott (eds) *Culture, Society and the Media,* Methuen, London: 56–90.

Hallin, D (1994) *We Keep America on Top of the World: Television Journalism and the Public Sphere*, Routledge, London and New York.

Hargreaves, I & Thomas, J (2002) *New News, Old News*, ITC and BSC, London.

Harris, M (1985) 'The ABC seedy? Certainly not', *Weekend Australian, Magazine*, 4–5 May: 10.

Harrison, T (1994) (ed.) *The Australian Film and Television Companion*, Simon and Schuster, Sydney.

Hartley, J (1992) *The Politics of Pictures: The Creation of the Public in the Age of Popular Media*, Routledge, London and New York.

—— (1996) *Popular Reality: Journalism, Modernity and Popular Culture*, Routledge, London.

—— (1999) *Uses of Television*, Routledge, London and New York.

Henderson, G (1991) 'For 8c, all the bias you can take', *Sydney Morning Herald*, 22 January: 12.

Henningham, J (1982) 'The people behind the news', *Bulletin*, 19 January: 74–75.

—— (1984) 'Australian television journalists' professional values and audience orientations', PhD dissertation, University of Queensland.

—— (1995) 'Political journalists' professional values', *Australian Journal of Political Science*, 30, 2: 321–334.

Hooks, B (1988) 'Kennedy light on for news', *Age*, 26 April: 14.

Horin, A (1978) 'The decline and fall of TDT', *National Times*, 19–24 June: 9–10.

Horrocks, R (2004) 'Turbulent television: the New Zealand experiment', *Television and New Media*, 5, 1, February: 55–68.

Inglis, K (1998) 'Whose ABC?', *Walkley Magazine*, July: 15.

Jauss, HR (1982) *Aesthetic Experience and Literary Hermeneutics*, trans. Michael Shaw, University of Minnesota Press, Minneapolis.

Katz, J (1994) 'The media's war on kids: from the Beatles to Beavis and Butt-head', *Rolling Stone*, February: 31, 33, 97.

Kellner, D (1995) *Media Culture: Cultural Studies, Identity and Politics Between the Modern and the Postmodern*, Routledge, London and New York.

Kevill, S (2002) *Beyond the Soundbite: BBC Research into Public Disillusion with Politics*, BBC, London.

Langer, J (1998) *Tabloid Television: Popular Journalism and the 'Other' News*, Routledge, London.

Littlemore, S (1996) *The Media and Me*, ABC Books, Sydney.

Lumby, C (1997) *Bad Girls: The Media, Sex and Feminism in the 90s*, Allen & Unwin, Sydney

—— (1999) *Gotcha! Life in a Tabloid World*, Allen & Unwin, Sydney.

Lyons, J (1988) 'In search of the real Robbo', *Weekend Australian Magazine*, 30 April–1 May: 3.

McAdam, A (1983) 'The ABC's Marxists', *Quadrant*, Jan/Feb: 53–61.

McGuigan, J (1992) *Cultural Populism*, Routledge, London.

Mackay, H (1999) *Turning Point: Australians Choosing their Future*, Pan Macmillan, Sydney.

McKee, A (2001) *Australian Television: A Genealogy of Great Moments*, Oxford University Press, Melbourne.

MacLean, S (2004a) 'Matilda waltzes into cynical politicians', *Australian*, 26 August: 43.

—— (2004b) 'Players primed for poll position', *Australian*, 2 September: 17.

—— (2004c) 'Journos seen as wrong, biased', *Australian*, 7 October: 18.

Madgwick, R (1969) 'For news accuracy, for entertainment quality, for public affairs impartiality', *Ausfact*, October: 14–17.

Malone, P (2003) 'Objective: objectivity', *Walkley Magazine*, 22: 16–17.

Marshall, PD (1997) *Celebrity and Power: Fame in Contemporary Culture*, University of Minnesota Press, Minneapolis.

Martin, F (2004) 'Net worth: the unlikely rise of ABC online' in G.Goggin (ed.) *Virtual Nation: The Internet in Australia*, UNSW Press, Sydney: 193–208.

Mascariotte, G-J (1991) 'C'mon girl: Oprah Winfrey and the discourse of feminine talk', *Genders*, 11, Fall: 81–110.

Masters, C (1992) *Inside Story*, Angus and Robertson, Sydney.

Mathieson, C & Meade, A (1998) 'Networks witness news turn-off', *Australian*, 24 August: 16.

Meade, A (1999) 'TV's tawdry affairs', *Australian, Media*, 22–28 April: 2–3.

—— (2002) 'Tired of frivolous affairs', *Australian, Media*, 12–18 September: 4–5.

—— (2004) 'Ray's not afraid of an old-fashioned street fight', *Australian, Media*, 15 July: 17.

Milliband, R (1978) 'A state of de-subordination', *British Journal of Sociology* 29, 4: 401–410.

Milliken, R (1977) 'This Day Tonight staggers towards its tenth birthday', *National Times*, 14–19 February: 14.

Mindich, D (2004) *Tuned Out: Why Young People don't Follow the News*, Oxford University Press, New York.

Moodie, A & J Della-Giacoma (1992) 'Audiences have a taste for TV news', *Australian*, 25 September: 5.

Moran, A (1985) *Images and Industry: Television Drama Production in Australia*, Currency Press, Sydney.

Moran, A & O'Regan, T (1989) (eds) *Australian Screen*, Penguin, Melbourne.

Morris, S (2004) 'Libel law may stifle debate', *Australian, Media*, 6 May: 17.

Munster, G (1971) 'Cracking down on TDT', *Nation*, 16 October: 5–6.

Murphy, D (1996) 'Facts and friction', *Bulletin*, May 28: 14–17.

Murphy, J (1988) 'The king reclaims his crown', *Age*, 29 February: 24.

O'Regan, T (1993) *Australian Television Culture*, Allen & Unwin, Sydney.

Peach, B (1992) *This Day Tonight: How Australian Current Affairs TV Came of Age*, ABC Books, Sydney.

Plane, T (1999) 'All the news that's fit to lampoon', *Australian, Media*, 8–14 April: 8–9.

Plunkett, R (1994) 'Strange times', *Age, Green Guide*, 10 March: 1–2.

Price, M (2003) 'Latham's interesting media maul', 11 December, 2003, <http://www.theaustralian.news.com.au/printpage/0,5942,8112114, 00.html>.

Accessed 13 December, 2003.

Raymond, R (1999) *Out of the Box: An Inside View of the Coming of Current Affairs and Documentaries to Australian Television*, Seaview Press, Henley, SA.

Redden, G (2003) 'Read the whole thing: journalism, weblogs and the re-mediation of the war in Iraq', *Media International Australia*, no. 109, November: 153–165.

Reid. P (2004) 'Bias monitoring could undermine the ABC's strengths', *Australian*, 11 November: 18.

Reines, R (1990) 'Jennifer Keyte: flying high', *Mode Australia*, July: 19–22.

Rennie, E & Young, S (2004) 'Park life: the commons and communications policy' in G.Goggin (ed.) *Virtual Nation: The Internet in Australia*, UNSW Press, Sydney: 242–257.

Ross, A (1989) *No Respect: Intellectuals and Popular Culture*, Routledge, New York.

Rowe, D (1994) 'Hard copy, soft porn' in S Cunningham & T Miller (eds) *Contemporary Australian Television*, UNSW Press, Sydney: 90–109.

Safe, M (1995) 'The disillusioned Steve Vizard', *Weekend Australian, Magazine*, 25–26 February: 34–37.

Shattuc. J (1997) *The Talking Cure: TV Talk Shows and Women*, Routledge, New York.

—— (1998) 'Go Ricki: politics, perversion and pleasure in the 1990s' in C Geraghty & D Lusted (eds) *The Television Studies Book*, Edward Arnold, London: 212–227.

Shipp, G (1971) 'The impartiality of TDT: pretence or reality?', *Quadrant*, May/June: 26–33.

Shipp, G & Tiffen, R (1991) 'The ABC and the Gulf War: Tiffen for the defence', *Current Affairs Bulletin*, 68, 3, August: 19–26.

Simper, E (1997) 'Not so much biased as bullied', *Australian*, 15 March: 52.

—— (1998) 'The ABC of muzzling', *Australian*, 30–31 May: 22.

—— (2004) 'ABC gives Coalition slim edge', *Australian*: 2 December, 18.

Sternberg, J (1995) 'Children of the information revolution: Generation X and the future of journalism', *CQU Working Papers in Communications and Cultural Studies*, 2: 45–59.

—— (2002) 'Youth media' in S Cunningham & G Turner (eds) *The Media and Communications in Australia*, Allen & Unwin, Sydney.

—— (2004) 'Generation X and Television Current Affairs: Journalism and Youth Culture in the 1990s', unpublished PhD dissertation, University of Queensland.

Stone, G (2000) *Compulsive Viewing*, Penguin, Melbourne.

Sweetapple, P (1985) 'Political bias denied by TV station director', *Australian*, 3 May: 2.

Tiffen, R (2000) 'Conflicts in the news: publicity interests, public images and political impacts' in H Tumber (ed.) *Media Power, Professionals and Policies*, Routledge, London: 190–205.

Tulloch, J & Turner, G (1989) (eds) *Australian Television: Programs, pleasures and politics*, Allen & Unwin, Sydney.

Turner, G (1989) 'Transgressive television: from *In Melbourne Tonight* to *Perfect Match*', in J Tulloch & G Turner (eds) *Australian Television: Programs, Pleasures and Politics*, Allen & Unwin, Sydney: 25–37.

—— (1994) *Making it National: Nationalism and Australian Popular Culture*, Allen & Unwin, Sydney.

—— (1996a) 'Maintaining the news', *Culture and Policy*, vol. 7, no. 3: 127–65.

—— (1996b) 'Current affairs hits the off button', *Australian*, 15 November: 17.

—— (1996c) 'Post-journalism: news and current affairs programming from the late 80s to the present', *Media International Australia*, no. 82, November:78–91.

—— (1997) 'First Contact: coming to terms with the cable guy', *UTS Review*, 3, 2: 109–121.

—— (1999) 'Tabloidisation, journalism and the possibility of critique', *International Journal of Cultural Studies*, 2,1: 59–76.

—— (2001) 'Sold out: recent shifts in television news and current affairs in Australia', in M Bromley (ed.), *No News is Bad News: Radio, Television and the Public*, Longman, Harlow: 46–58.

—— (2003) 'Popularising politics: *This Day Tonight* and Australian television current affairs', *Media International Australia*, no.106, February: 137–150.

—— (2004) *Understanding Celebrity*, Sage, London.

Turner, G, Bonner, F & Marshall, PD (2000) *Fame Games: The Production of Celebrity in Australia*, Cambridge University Press, Cambridge.

Turner, G & Cunningham, S (2000) (eds) *The Australian TV Book*, Allen & Unwin, Sydney.

TV Times (1969) [no byline] 'ABC Chairman attacks current affairs critics', 6 August: 17.

Walter, J (1996) *Tunnel Vision: The Failure of Political Imagination*, Allen & Unwin, Sydney.

Wark, M (1994) *Virtual Geography: Living with Global Media Events*, University of Indiana Press, Bloomington.

West, DM & Orman, J (2003) *Celebrity Politics*, Prentice Hall, Upper Saddle River, NJ.

White, M (1992) *Tele-Advising: Therapeutic Discourse in American Television*, University of North Carolina Press, Chapel Hill.

Whitley, P (1988) 'Nervous king fights for news crown', *Australian*, 28 April: 13.

Williams, R (1974) *Television: Technology and Cultural Form*, Fontana Collins, London.

Williams, S (1994) 'Current affairs coverage under seige', *Australian*, 6 June: 12.

—— (1996) 'Late starters time it just right', *Australian*, 2 February: 21.

Wilmoth, P & Button, J (1990) 'News wars: or is it entertainment tonight?' *Age*, Saturday Extra, 'News Wars Supplement', 28 April: 1. 6.

Wilson, T (1994) 'Television and difference: address, audience and anticipations of narrative', *Australian Journal of Communication*, 21, 1: 33–45.

Woodham, A (1974) 'Bill Peach: TV's Mr Nice Guy', *Cleo*, January: 64–66.

Zawawi, C (1994) 'Sources of news: who feeds the watchdog?' *Australian Journalism Review*, 16, 1: 67–71.

Index